MISSIONARY STRATEGIES

RHEMA Ministerial
Association International

First Printing 1995
ISBN 0-89276-957-2

In the U.S. write:
Kenneth Hagin Ministries
P.O. Box 50126
Tulsa, OK 74150-0126

In Canada write:
Kenneth Hagin Ministries
P.O. Box 335, Station D
Etobicoke (Toronto), Ontario
Canada, M9A 4X3

Contents

RHEMA Ministerial Association International

P.O. Box 50126 • Tulsa, OK 74150-0126 • (918) 258-1588

Dear Friend:

It is a great pleasure to present this manual in which RMAI missionaries share both spiritual and natural aspects regarding their ministries. It has been a tremendous joy to see hundreds of men and women attend RHEMA Bible Training Center and then go on to fulfill the call of God on their lives by reaching out to people in other countries.

The contributors to this manual are RHEMA graduates who are ordained members of the RHEMA Ministerial Association International. They are all full-time missionaries living in various parts of the world. All of these individuals have had to adapt to different cultures and customs, and some of them live in remote, underdeveloped nations. They also vary in levels of experience; some have been in missions for many years, while others are newer on the field.

We desire that the information in this manual be of great benefit to others who will follow in the steps of these missionaries in taking the Gospel of the Lord Jesus Christ to the ends of the earth. It is also our prayer that many pastors will take the time to read these accounts and be challenged to increase their involvement with missions and missionaries. As pastors, our responsibilities reach beyond our local congregations, and it is by joining forces with missionaries through financial and prayer support that we are able to not only impact our own communities, but also the world.

As you read this manual, please keep in mind that what the different contributors have shared is how they feel God led *them*. Please remember that what works in one ministry or ministry setting might not be effective in another. This is why we stress so heavily at RHEMA Bible Training Center that ministers learn how to be led by the Spirit of God *themselves* and not just imitate someone else.

As you read the following pages, we trust you will be inspired, instructed, edified, and challenged! And may the Church ever be mindful of and obedient to its commission: *". . .Go ye into all the world, and preach the gospel to every creature"* (Mark 16:15).

Yours in Christ,

Rev. Kenneth Hagin Jr.
RMAI International Director

Chapter 1

Being a Missionary in a Primitive Setting

By Dennis Cook ('79 '80)

Dennis and Jeanne Cook are both 1980 graduates of RHEMA Bible Training Center in Broken Arrow, Oklahoma, and founders of Vida Ministries in Panama, South-Central America.

Upon graduation from RHEMA, Dennis served as an assistant pastor for 18 months in a small church in Kokomo, Indiana. In November 1981, Dennis, Jeanne, and their four children left the United States to work in a leper colony in Panama. After two years at the colony, God called Dennis and Jeanne to work among the Choco Indians in the Darien jungle of Panama. After 10 years of ministry in the Darien jungle, the Cooks now oversee eight churches in South-Central America.

The Cooks' youngest child, Chad, age 21, is working with them in Panama. Their other children, Chris, 26, Jennifer, 25, and Jason, 23, along with the Cooks' two grandchildren, Brittany, 4, and Kristen, 1, reside in the United States.

Shortly after I was saved, I heard a missionary speak at a Charismatic church meeting. After hearing him speak, I remember saying that I would like to do something for the Lord similar to what he was doing. After I received the baptism of the Holy Spirit, I worked as a lay-leader in two Bible-study groups. I was content to do whatever I could put my hand to for the Lord. Later, my brother and I and another gentleman started a small church.

Then in 1977, the United States was debating the Carter-Torrijos Treaty, which dealt with Panama Canal territory. It was during this time that I read an article in the newspaper about a leper colony in Panama, and the Lord spoke to me to pray for the people there!

My wife and I made it a practice to set aside time every night to worship the Lord (not asking for anything; only giving thanks and adoration to Him). During that time of worship, three days after the Lord had instructed me to pray for people in the leper colony, I had a vision. In the vision, I saw a man disembarking from an airplane in Panama and going to a leper colony and preaching the Gospel!

Although my wife did not see the vision, we both received joy in our spirits simultaneously as I witnessed what had taken place in the vision. We both assumed that the Lord had sent someone as a laborer to these dear people, so we continued to worship Him and give thanks for His love and faithfulness.

Soon afterward, Rev. Kenneth E. Hagin held a seminar in Indianapolis, Indiana, and we attended every service. It was during that meeting that the Lord put it on our hearts to study after Brother

Hagin. We were thinking more along the line of enrolling in RHEMA's Correspondence Bible School, but the Lord directed us to attend RHEMA Bible Training Center for two years.

That was not an easy decision for us. We were living in our first home, we had four children, three of whom were in school, and I had 13 years' seniority at a good-paying job. But we made the right decision in attending RHEMA. It always pays to obey God.

During our first year at RHEMA, we received so much rich teaching that we wondered if we would be able to remember it all! The Lord also began to reveal to us more and more of His plan for our lives. For instance, during another time of worship at home, the Holy Spirit revealed that the man in the vision I had seen getting off that plane in Panama was me!

Jeanne and I then knew that we would eventually be working in Panama. After this time, whenever we would hear a missionary speak, our spirits would just sob and cry out for the lost world.

After graduation from RHEMA and a brief 10-day visit to Guatemala, we returned to Indiana to work in the church we had helped begin two and a half years earlier. During the next 18 months that we served the Lord there, we learned a lot about the ministry.

Preparing for the Mission Field

After six months in Indiana, the Lord told us to get prepared because we would be leaving within a year. We paid all of our existing bills, getting out of debt. We corresponded with every ministry we knew of (with no success), trying to find a contact in Panama.

There were many obstacles and hindrances. We battled resistance from parents who couldn't understand why their grandchildren were being dragged to a "God-forsaken" foreign country to suffer, starve, and be tortured! We also wrote to two world leprosy organizations to find out more about the colony in Panama. Both organizations responded that they didn't know of a leper colony in Panama, and if we found one to inform *them*!

Raising support can also be very discouraging for a new missionary. In fact, doing this part of the ministry has defeated many God-called missionaries even before they stepped foot on foreign soil.

I visited many churches, trying to raise support for the vision the Lord had put into my heart. A few churches, friends, and people with whom we attended RHEMA promised to support us. That amounted to about $350 a month.

When the year was up and it was time to go to Panama as the Lord had said, we were fully out of debt and had purchased our airplane tickets. Our home church promised to pray for us and handle our finances. (You need a home church to which you are accountable and where you can be "covered" by their prayers.) So on November 30, 1981, our family left for Panama with $1,000 in our pockets, 29 pieces of luggage, and peace in our hearts.

Experiencing the Supernatural: God's Grace for Paying the Price

Before we even stepped on the plane to go to Panama, the Lord had told me that we would work in the leper colony, among the American military, and with the Panamanian people. We needed that encouragement for what was ahead.

When we arrived in Panama, we were ill-prepared. We could not speak the language, had little money, did not know anyone, and in the natural, didn't even know if the leper colony really existed! All we had was the "rhema" of God's Word and His peace in our hearts.

But God answered our faith because within three days, we were pastors of the English-speaking part of a church located in an off-post military housing area — and only five miles from the leper colony!

Our rent was $350 a month. Since we only brought $1,000 with us, it wasn't long before we were in need of a miracle. Basically, we did not have enough money to *exist*, let alone to minister.

However, our Father God is in the *providing* business, and we witnessed the miraculous during that time! For instance, one time when there was no food in the house, the Lord supernaturally provided food for us — three times a day for three days.

After we would eat a meal, Jeanne would put an almost empty pot back into the refrigerator, and God would supernaturally fill it up! We ate the same kind of food for nine straight meals, but at least we had eaten! After three days, we received a check in the mail. Later that day when we went to eat out of the pot, the food was not there!

Although we had no means of transportation for the first year and a half we were in Panama, the Lord provided us the strength and grace to walk through the rain (the average rainfall is 150 inches a year in Panama) and extreme heat (up to 120 degrees) to minister to the people of the leper colony.

When we first arrived in Panama, we did whatever we could find to put our hands to. We conducted Bible studies among the American military, pastored a small church, evangelized our community, and worked with a Panamanian church.

These outreaches helped us become known among the people and allowed the Holy Spirit to speak to people's hearts to help us financially, materially, emotionally, and so forth.

As a minister of the Gospel, especially as an overseas missionary, try to find people to fellowship with who believe like you do, but do not rule out those in the ministry who are "outside" your camp in the sense that they don't have the understanding of the Word of God that you do. We found out that what Rev. Kenneth Hagin Jr. taught us at RHEMA was true: You can learn *something* from just about anyone. (We also learned from his "spelling class" that success in the ministry is spelled *w-o-r-k*!)

The first day we arrived at Palo Seco, the leper colony, I was amazed that it looked exactly as it appeared in the vision — and with exactly the same people I had seen in the vision!

Religious people in Panama had told these people that their affliction was their cross to bear for God's glory. When we would tell them that God loved them, they would show us the affected parts of their bodies and say sarcastically, "Yeah, He really loves me."

It took many months of loving these people and sharing the Word of God with them before they allowed us to pray for them. And even then, they would only allow us to pray for minor ailments. After many manifestations of healing, however, they finally allowed us to pray for their healing of leprosy.

While we were working with the leper colony and a local Panamanian church, we heard about the Choco Indians in the Darien jungle. We made a couple of visits to the jungle and knew in our hearts that God was moving us in this direction. Under normal circumstances, God will not instruct a leader of a church or group to leave that church or position without first replacing him. A flock without a pastor or leader is in danger. But the Lord had already begun to bring others from the American military community to work among the people of the leper colony. As we trained the Americans, we knew their hearts were full of love for God and these people. Before we moved into the Darien jungle, all the people in the leper colony were saved, and many were healed!

There are many differences between what we call big-city missions and primitive missions. In primitive missions, you lack many conveniences such as electricity, water, roads, communications, schools for the children, hospitals, transportation, and fellowship with people on your own level of ministry.

When the Lord directed us to go into the jungle (*National Geographic* says it contains some of the densest jungle in the world), we knew that we had to "toughen up" and rely more on the ability of God than on our own ability. Our first course of action was to visit different places in the jungle and to develop relationships among the Indians.

The Forerunner to Ministry: Building Trust

We spent one year getting to know these people and helping them in many ways (usually materially and practically) before we ever held a Gospel campaign. We ate with the Indians, slept in their huts, worked in the mud with them, and listened to them. We ministered on an individual basis because we wanted them to personally know our hearts.

When we decided to have our first open-air campaign, we were received with open arms because the people knew we wanted only the best for them. We had established our motives by our actions and deeds. And God was faithful to establish *us* by proving and confirming His Word with manifestations of signs and wonders. Many new births and healings took place. And in one case, three witches who tried to disrupt the campaign were blinded! After the witches repented, the Lord restored their sight, and they received Him as their Savior!

We determined not to compete with any other work or church in any given area or location. If a certain area already had a work in progress, we would offer our help but would look for another place to start evangelizing and developing a body of believers.

Although there were many churches in the jungle, they were for the Panamanians and the Colombians, but not for the Choco Indians. Since there was no work among the Indians, we started sharing the Gospel with them. I was asked many times by other pastors in the area why we wasted our time with the Indians. These pastors said that the Indians were too hard to teach and that it was very difficult to reach their villages. "Why not use your time more effectively with the Panamanians?" they'd ask.

But God did not say to go into all the world and preach the Gospel when things are easy! He said to go into all the world and preach to *every creature*!

Also, things were not easy for us because we were not representing a denomination. We had to prove ourselves to the other ministers as well as to the Indians. One time the Indians told us that because there were no Bibles in their dialects, they were going to watch us, and we would be their Bible! What pressure!

The ministry of a missionary is a unique calling. A person whom God uses in this type of ministry will operate to some extent in each of the fivefold ministries. Following the example of Jesus, we started discipling a few Indians and endeavored to place within them the vision to reach their own people.

This required us to live among them, so we rented a piece of land and pitched our tents! After our financial support started to grow, we bought the land and began to build our own house.

We lived in tents for one and a half years before we laid the foundations for our house. After eight years of living without electricity and running water, we finally completed and moved into our house!

Soon it became apparent that we needed a way of educating those God was calling into the ministry, so we started a Bible school on our land and began with seven students. Two years later, we graduated six of these people.

We learned that the location of the school hindered many from attending, so we began holding Bible schools in the villages. This required me to do a lot of traveling by many modes of transportation — by car, motorcycle, boat, horse, and on foot! In one case, I walked 15 miles twice a week to one of the villages. Even to this day, I sometimes make that walk. When you're compelled by the love of God for people, you will experience His grace to overcome many types of inconveniences.

Family First: Establishing Priorities On the Mission Field

During this time of ministry in the jungle, other considerations had to be addressed. One of these was the education of our children. After we came to Panama, we found it necessary to home-school our children. This decision takes a lot of commitment on the part of both the parents and the children, but we had no other alternative since the schools in the jungle were only for children up to the sixth grade, and the quality of the education was very poor.

A pastor in Indiana had heard my wife and children share our testimony on television and was moved by the honesty of the children's response to the host's questions about missionary life. This pastor offered to help us with a formal program to educate the kids. This required my wife to become, among other things, a full-time teacher. She and the children spent practically 24 hours a day together, and there were many challenges to overcome.

Although our support continued to increase as we continued to do our part in the ministry, the conveniences for my family did not improve. There was a time during which I neglected my family's needs in order to meet the ministry's needs as well as the needs of the Indians. I was concerned about what my supporters would think if I spent any money on my family. *This type of thinking is wrong!*

Don't neglect your family for the sake of the ministry. Your family is your *first* responsibility. Provide the best you can for their comfort and needs.

During our first eight years on the mission field, we did not have a salary, and I spent just enough of the support money to barely provide for my family. I used the rest for the ministry. When my children returned to the States to enter college, we were forced to take a salary in order for them to qualify for educational aid. (By the way, one of my sons scored among the top 10 percent in the nation on his S.A.T. exam.)

Sharing Your Vision
And Raising Support

In order to increase your base of support, you must expose your part of the ministry of Jesus Christ to prospective supporters. So in order to let people know more fully what God had called us to do, we decided to return to the States about every two years to raise support.

The first time I returned was a nightmare! Most of the letters I had sent to churches to schedule meetings had not made it through the Panamanian mail system. I knew very few pastors to contact to try and get meetings. I found out that most pastors receive many requests to have a visiting speaker come to their church and can't possibly fulfill them all. Also, the most inefficient form of communication to schedule meetings is by mail.

The result of my first attempt was dismal. I spent a lot more money traveling and staying in the States than I raised in support. However, God is faithful, and a pastor offered to set up my itinerary the next time I was in the States.

It is important that you have someone in the States who loves you and will arrange meetings for you! Because of this pastor's help in setting up our itinerary, our times spent in the States have become very fruitful.

A common mistake many missionaries make is to develop an attitude that the churches are *obligated* to support them. But God is the One who called you. *He* sent you, and *He* will speak to the churches He wants to participate in His work.

We rely upon the Holy Spirit to speak to the hearts of the people who are to be a part of the work in Panama. Your part as a missionary is to expose the ministry to as many people as possible. God's part is to speak to the hearts of those He wants involved.

Another common mistake missionaries make is using all of their time Stateside to raise support. Doing this will not refresh you because when you're raising support, you're always giving out and not receiving encouragement for your spirit man. Also, your family will start to resent the ministry because there is no time for them just for relaxing and getting refreshed.

I encourage all missionaries who are graduates of RHEMA to try to attend one or more RHEMA meetings whether it is a regional meeting or a meeting in Tulsa. And do something special with your family that does not involve ministry. Splurge on them a little. Your supporters will understand.

To maintain your support, you should communicate to the supporters on a regular basis. We began by writing a one-page handwritten letter to our supporters monthly. This also included a black-and-white photograph of the work we had started in Panama.

As we could, we increased the correspondence to include a monthly newsletter that we sent to anyone who wished to receive it. We followed what we had learned at RHEMA about publications. As we could, we upgraded the quality. We always made the newsletter personal and included only truthful news.

There is a temptation to direct the focus of your ministry in such a way that it produces more exciting news for your newsletter. *Don't do it!* Although the opportunity is available to compete for the

Christian dollar for your support, you are to be led by the Holy Spirit and to place your faith in God for your support.

You are responsible for fulfilling what God has called you to do and not to impress man or live up to someone else's expectations. The people to whom God has spoken to support your part of His ministry will be faithful to Him. So put your faith in Him and do only as *He* directs.

As you continue your work for the Lord, your ministry will develop in many different areas, one of which will be your relationship with the local community. For example, when we first arrived in the Darien jungle, we didn't have much of a relationship with the community, especially with public officials. We were constantly harassed by the police and the military.

We have been shot at twice, detained by the police a few times, and I was put on trial once by a nonbelieving village chief in an attempt to rid the area of our church and the Christian influence.

In that situation, the people of the village, both believers and nonbelievers, rallied to my side! The result was that the court threw out the nonbelieving chief and made the pastor of our church the new chief of the village!

Now, however, we have favor with the local police. We help the local medical clinic, participate in and help with different village functions, and mix with the people. The Lord had spoken to us early on as we began our work in the jungle to develop good relations with both the Christians and the non-Christians in the community. This worked to our favor many times, as the people where we lived would warn us of plans to rob our house or cause other harm.

One time during the Noriega years, we received information that the military was going to come for us. With the help of the local community, we made plans to escape through the jungle to Colombia. Praise God, we did not have to execute our escape plan, but we are thankful for the people who were willing to help us.

Be Teachable When God Asks You To Expand Your Vision

As the ministry grew, we had to expand our operations. We conferred with leaders, read books about leadership, and even made decisions to change our personalities in areas that hindered us from growing with the ministry and becoming the leaders God called us to be. We simply enlarged our vision!

We eventually incorporated our ministry in the States to take the burden off the church that had for many years handled our office business. We now have a tax agent who does all of our ministry and personal taxes so we are not burdened down by the changing laws. We purchased tapes and books to instruct us in many areas that were new to us in the ministry.

When our children were with us, Jeanne's role in the ministry was very important and many-faceted. She was wife, mother, host, teacher, and prayer warrior. She listened, encouraged, and prayed. She worked from sunup to sundown without recognition. She did all the correspondence, sometimes up to 90 letters a month by hand, and planned the group trips and pastors' conferences. She wore many hats.

Now that our kids are grown, she travels with me and continues to function in many of the same capacities as before. Men, your wives are your "right arm." Appreciate their input to the ministry. Without their participation, you cannot be successful.

The following are important suggestions for those who believe they are called to the mission field:

1. **Know that you are called to be a missionary.**

   As Christians we are called to live by faith. And without faith we can't please God. If you don't *know* that you are called, then you are not in faith. Many times, it is the *knowing* that puts you over.

2. **After graduation from Bible school, find a ministry where you can work to prove your faithfulness to the ministry. During this time you can complete many of the other suggestions.**

   Ask for the job in the church or ministry that no other person wants to do and then do it faithfully. If you are not willing to work in the jobs that are least desirable, then you probably will not make it on the mission field. There are clear, scriptural guidelines for people who want to enter into the ministry.

   Also, remember that God is not in a hurry. If He needed you to be somewhere sooner, then He would have called you sooner. Don't be *driven* to do something; instead, be led by the Holy Spirit. Pressure to perform usually leads to mistakes. However, don't waste the time that you have to prepare yourself.

3. **Investigate the country.**

   If you know what country you are being called to, visit that country to learn about the laws, customs, cost of living, and so forth. Sometimes this will require more than one visit. If you are not sure about which country you are called to, take trips to various countries to allow God to speak to your heart. *If you don't have a love for the people of that country, then you are not being called to that country.* RHEMA and other organizations offer opportunities to visit the mission field.

4. **Begin to learn the language, and learn about such things as construction, mechanics, water systems, and medicines.**

   All the natural areas in which you develop will save you time, money, and frustration when you are in a primitive area. There are some organizations that will prepare you to live in a primitive area.

5. **Get out of debt.**

6. **Find someone to handle your finances, correspondence, and general office requirements.**

   Whomever you choose, make sure that they really love you and are totally behind you. In handling your business affairs, they will be committing themselves to a great deal of important work on your behalf.

7. **If you have children and will be ministering in a primitive setting, prepare for home-schooling.**

   Find someone who will let you work through their church school to buy materials and to confer graduation certificates.

8. **Raise a "more than sufficient" level of support *before* you go to the field.**

This is perhaps one of the most difficult areas, but one in which God's grace is sufficient. Talk to friends and other ministers, visit other churches or Bible studies, and go anywhere to share your vision and raise support.

Your previous trips to the country will help prove your commitment to live there. When the Lord gives you a date, announce it, and work toward leaving on that date. Remember, you will have immediate expenses upon entering the country, so go prepared with plenty of money to get established physically and *legally*.

9. **If you can, find an organization in that country with whom you can work. If not, find an area without a work and begin one there.**

In whatever situation, cooperate with other churches and ministries. Do not compete with them; there are plenty of unsaved people to go around! You can save a lot of time, money, and frustration by gleaning and learning from another ministry that is already established in that country.

The following are several suggestions once you have become established in a country:

1. **Develop and maintain a regular personal correspondence with your supporters.**

Put the best quality into your correspondence that you can afford. People judge you on the quality of your newsletter. Try to include a picture or pictures of your work.

2. **Obey the laws of the land.**

To violate the laws just for the sake of convenience is against the Scriptures and should never be done (Rom. 13:1-5). This includes paying bribes. You are a representative of God, and your actions should always represent His actions.

I am not saying that you should not receive it as from God if an official who has the authority to make exceptions grants you favor. I *am* saying that you should never *initiate* the action by offering some form of inappropriate compensation.

Also, should a government change politically, if you are legal and ethical in all of your activities both past and present, you will stand a better chance of remaining in the country.

3. **Don't preach *against* anything, but preach the *Gospel*.**

We have found favor with the chiefs and heads of the Indian reservation because we do not preach against their traditions. Others who had come here before us told the people that it was a sin to wear loincloths, to eat pork, and for the women to be bare-breasted. These people said the men had to wear long-sleeve shirts and so forth. But if you simply preach the Word of God, the Holy Spirit will convict the people in their heart to change customs that are not pleasing to Him.

4. **Get to know your people and never have an attitude of superiority.**

We have learned many valuable lessons from the Indians about living in and traveling through the jungle that we could not otherwise have learned if we had not kept the lines of communication open.

5. **Always guard and maintain your family well.**

In most cases, women and children will pay a higher price than men when entering a primitive type of ministry. Remember, you will be your family's pastor in spiritual things. Teach them, encourage them, and pray for and together with them. Never be too busy for them. *Do not sacrifice your family for the ministry.*

6. **Always keep your vision before you and remember that it is God you are to please.**

You will receive unfair criticism about your motives, about how you use the ministry money as well as your own personal money, and about what types of outreaches you have. I believe there is usually a small amount of truth in every criticism, so I look for that, change what needs to be changed, and forget the rest.

7. **Realize and be prepared for the fact that in many cases the people to whom you will be ministering will be illiterate and ignorant.**

You will need a lot of patience and faith before you start to see spiritual growth. For example, you may need to teach the people how to read before you can teach them the Bible.

You must become simple, repetitive, and basic in your teaching of the Word of God.

8. **Remember that God has faith in you!**

God knows *where* He is going to send you, *when* He is going to send you, and He is acquainted with your abilities. Keep in continual communication with God through prayer and the Word, and His grace will see you through!

Chapter 2

Pioneering Missions in a Foreign Land

By Ed ('83 '84) and Laurie Elliott

Ed Elliott is the founder and director of Word of Life World Outreach. He has been working and living in Africa with his wife, Laurie, and his sons (Eddie, age 6, and Chase, age 2) for more than 10 years since his graduation from RHEMA Bible Training Center in 1984. Laurie is a graduate of Oral Roberts University in Tulsa. The Elliotts' mission base is located just outside of Johannesburg, South Africa.

Ed's ministry takes him and his team throughout southern and central Africa, evangelizing and teaching. In 1992, the president of Zambia invited Ed to preach at an independence celebration that was broadcast live across the nation. Ed has also traveled into the countries of Zimbabwe, Mozambique, Namibia, Botswana, Swaziland, Malawi, and South Africa, holding crusades and establishing churches.

When you accept the challenge of going to the mission field to pioneer a new work, you will walk into one of the most exciting adventures of your life! You and the people you minister to will never be the same! Daily, you will encounter opportunities for victory, but not without a few challenges.

During the past 10 years, my wife and I have had the privilege of seeing more than 2,000,000 people come to know Jesus Christ as their Lord and Savior and of assisting in pioneering more than 40 churches. We have seen more than 50,000 people baptized in the Holy Ghost at one time. We have also seen amazing healings and numerous miracles take place.

I am sharing this with you, not to boast about what we have done, but to show how God will use you to do great and mighty works that you may have never thought possible.

I believe that missions is epitomized in the story of the 12 spies found in Numbers chapter 13. When you respond to the call of God to become a missionary and go to a foreign land, your success will be based not on how much money you have raised or how many people are praying for you, or even whether you have a prophetic word from God. It will be based on how well you know God and know who you are as His son or daughter.

Develop a Pioneering Spirit

NUMBERS 13:30

30 And Caleb stilled the people before Moses, and said, Let us go up at once, and possess it; for we are well able to overcome it.

To be successful in your ministry, you will need to have the same spirit that Joshua and Caleb had. There will be many who will tell you, "It cannot be done!" "The people's hearts are hard!" or "No one has ever had any success in that place!"

Even well-meaning family members will try to convince you that you are making a serious mistake by going to the mission field. These voices will be telling you about the giants in the land and why it would be better to stay where you are.

Since becoming a Christian, I have had a burning desire to see people saved and come to the knowledge of how good God is. I also sensed from the beginning that I would work in foreign lands preaching the Gospel.

While I was attending RHEMA Bible Training Center, that desire and hunger continued to increase. And as graduation drew close, I began to seek the Lord in prayer about the next step of direction for my life.

One afternoon while praying and discussing this with the Lord, He spoke to me very clearly and said, "I am going to send you to Zimbabwe and Mozambique." He also told me that He was going to send me there in October and November. I knew these countries were in Africa but I had to find them on the map!

Getting From 'Here' to 'There'

I was excited at what God was doing, but wondered how God was going to put the whole thing together. At the time, all I could do was to pray and trust the Lord. About two weeks later, a friend introduced me to a couple of men from Zimbabwe who were doing a lot of mission work in Mozambique.

After an evening of fellowship, they asked if I would like to come to Africa and help them with their work. I said that I would love to and asked them when they would like me to come. They looked at each other and said, "How about October and November?" I told them to expect me!

When I left those men that night, I was so thrilled to see the hand of God at work, but I also realized I had a lot of work to do. I had to get a passport, visas, immunizations, plane reservations, and do a good degree of research about the nations I was about to visit.

After some research, I found out I needed to bring medication to prevent malaria. All these things are important to find out about when going to the mission field.

The biggest hurdle for most people going to the mission field will be finances, and I was no exception. My wife, Laurie, and I were putting ourselves through school by waiting tables at a restaurant. Like most students, we did not have an abundance of money floating around for me to fly to Africa for a couple of months. This would be the first great miracle we would see God do to get me to Africa.

Before I share this testimony, let me first point out what I believe to be a very important spiritual point. Psalm 127:1 says, *"Except the Lord build the house, they labour in vain that build it. . . ."*

Whatever the Lord calls you to do for Him, He will labor with you. He will open doors that need to be opened and put you in contact with people who will assist you in fulfilling your vision. Favor, blessing, and divine inspiration are all just a small part of how God works with you. The Scripture says, *". . .Not by might, nor by power, but by my spirit, saith the Lord of hosts"* (Zech. 4:6). The work of God will be accomplished as we develop a constant dependence on the work of the Holy Ghost.

Over the years, my wife and I have observed other missionaries laboring in vain. There seems to be no divine hookup. The favor of God seems to be absent, and they are always struggling for provision. They also suffer constant attacks and have very little success and victory in their mission work.

Years ago, I heard a very successful missionary say, "When God tells me to do something, God will pay. But when I say *I* am going to do something, then God lets *me* pay!"

Make sure you are following God's plan for your life! When you labor in vain, you will grow weary and tired and have to fight bitterness and jealousy as others around you succeed. You are too valuable to the Kingdom of God to waste your time in years of toil that produce very little fruit for our Heavenly Father.

The great victories my wife and I have seen on the mission field could not have come about without divine intervention. God's strength, favor, wisdom, and provision were all needed to accomplish our work for Him.

As I mentioned earlier, one of the biggest obstacles to reaching the mission field is finances. We had seen God provide to get us to Tulsa to go to Bible school, and He had supernaturally taken care of us. But now we needed a tremendous amount of money for my upcoming trip to Africa, plus additional funds to cover expenses while I would be away.

One afternoon while praying and discussing this with the Lord, He spoke to me that I was to save every penny over $50 that my wife and I made in tips each evening at our jobs. I shared this with my wife, and we were a bit perplexed, because very rarely did we make more than $50 in tips with the exception of the weekends! Even on weekends, it did not usually exceed $60.

During the week, we usually made between $25 and $30 an evening in tips. So we were wondering how saving about $20 a week could ever pay for my trip to Africa, especially since I would be leaving in about six months. There is not much you can do in a situation like that but just trust God and stay in faith!

That night after the Lord spoke to me, Laurie and I both went to work. It was Monday, which was usually the slowest night of the week. Business was good that night, and the tips were good, but seemingly not very much out of the ordinary. When we came home and began to count our tips, we were surprised to see that I made $76, and Laurie made $84! We were so excited — we thanked and praised God for what He was doing in our lives!

From that point on, we never made less then $50 per evening. When some of our regular customers found out that I was planning a mission trip to Africa, they would just hand me $20. We began to see God work in a wonderful way, providing the finances to make the trip and to cover our bills while I would be away.

Many times the will of God is progressive, and as you begin to walk it out in your own life, it comes more into focus. For example, we are doing things today in our ministry that I only had a glimpse of years ago. As you are obedient to follow the call of God on your life, your vision for ministry will be greatly defined. Acts 9:6 says, ". . .Lord, what wilt thou have me to do? And the Lord said unto him, Arise, and go into the city, and it shall be told thee what thou must do."

I was all eyes and ears when I arrived in Zimbabwe to help the missionaries who invited me. I wanted to learn from these men, and they taught me a lot that has helped me over the years.

Stay Focused and Committed to Your Vision

While I was in Mozambique, the Lord again spoke to me about my call and the purpose for my life. He told me that He had called me to southern and central Africa and that He would bring me into cities, towns, villages, and refugee camps where I would preach and teach His Word. He told me that multitudes would receive Him and that soon after I left, many of these people would die because of disease, drought, famine, and war but that I was not to weep or shed a tear because they would be with Him.

Over the years, I have seen the fulfillment of this word many times. My heart is full of joy because I know that many of the people I have preached to are now in the Presence of the Lord.

The eternal destiny of the people you are reaching should always be your focus. I have watched missionaries get caught up in meeting the social and physical needs of the people. Because they lost their focus, and many times their love for the things of God, they no longer desired to share these truths with the people.

Some missionaries are so involved in these social programs that they eventually have no time to do what God called them to do in the first place. The enemy can be very subtle in seducing you and leading you away from your vision. After all, as long as you are still helping people, you feel that you are in the will of God for your life.

Please do not misunderstand what I am saying. I believe it's important to minister to every area of a person's needs, and our ministry has done that for years. But *first*, we are called to minister the Gospel. Everything we do is aimed at bringing people to the knowledge of Jesus Christ as their Lord and Savior.

Always stay focused and totally committed to your vision, and do not allow yourself to be sidetracked.

Pioneering a New Work

When you determine where God is leading you to start a new work, there are many things to be considered.

1. **Learn the country's requirements for living and working in that country.**

    A. **Visas and work permits.** Research the many different types of visas and work permits that are available to you. Ask how long the country's government will allow you to stay in their country and whether the visas and work permits are renewable.

    Conditions are different for a tourist visa than they are for a resident or work visa. You might find you will need a combination of visas and permits to do what God is calling you to do. You can easily find this information by contacting the country's embassy here in the U.S.

    B. **Finances.** Some countries require a financial statement showing how much money you will be bringing into their country. Find out what they require. When you visit the country in which you intend to work, all of this can be better researched. We will discuss finances in greater detail later in the chapter.

    Over the years, my wife and I have transferred money almost every conceivable way from the U.S. to Africa. Let me share with you some practical advice that will save you a lot of aggravation. If you have not developed a good credit rating here in the U.S., then go to work right away to correct that and secure yourself a Visa, Mastercard, and American Express card.

One of the best ways to transfer money is through cash advances because they are a relatively safe, quick, and effective way of sending over your monthly support. Find a good bank in your area that has international connections, experience in wire transfers, and accepts your major credit cards. Some banks offer a lower exchange rate than others, so do your research well, and it can save you money.

2. Choose a location for your mission base.

    A. People. Access to the people you are called to reach should be one of your main considerations.

    B. Equipment. Can you get what you need to do your work, such as supplies, spare parts, food, Bibles, etc.? Try to purchase in the foreign country as much as you can of the equipment you will need. It will bless their economy, and you will have quicker access to spare parts.

    Waiting for parts to come from America can cost you weeks or months of valuable time. It might cost more to buy the product in that country, but in the long run, you will save.

    I know missionaries who had special trucks and Jeeps shipped out of America or their native country, but the country in which they were ministering also sold very adequate transportation. Then these missionaries were stranded for weeks doing nothing because of a breakdown. They had to order the necessary parts from their native country. This would not have been the case had they bought their vehicles locally.

    C. Accommodations. Is the housing available, affordable, and livable? When we moved to Africa to set up our base of operations, our financial picture was very unclear. We knew people had committed to support us, but many of them did not specify an amount. We found the most inexpensive house to rent and did all we could to keep our expenses down to a minimum.

    Eventually, we were able to determine our monthly support, and from that, we were able to begin to develop a budget.

    D. Communications. Communications are often overlooked when deciding on a location for a base. It is important for our ministry to have a telephone and a fax line, not just to communicate with our home office, but also with others around Africa when planning our work and outreaches.

    Many times a fax machine has saved us a long drive or days of waiting for a valuable document that we needed for traveling. Make the purchase of a fax machine a top priority item for your office on the field.

    E. Functional needs. Schooling, transportation, and hospitals all need to be considered when choosing a sight for your mission base. These needs will vary with different types of ministries. Our ministry requires a lot of travel both by road and air, so it is important that we have access to an airport.

    We also use a lot of technical equipment in our work, so it is important to us that we are able to service and maintain this equipment at all times and sometimes at short notice. I have had to fly specialized sound-equipment parts from the U.S. for quick repairs so we could maintain our crusade schedule.

So, as you can see, the location of your mission base is an important decision that needs to be researched thoroughly to maximize your potential and effectiveness for the Kingdom of God.

3. **Spy out the land.**

A. **Reconnaissance.** Before battles in the military are fought, a reconnaissance team is sent out to assess the strength of the enemy and to get a clear picture of the country that is going to be invaded. Reconnaissance is a tactical study designed to acquire as much information as possible before an attack is launched.

NUMBERS 13:1,2,17-20

1 And the Lord spake unto Moses, saying,

2 Send thou men, that they may search the land of Canaan, which I give unto the children of Israel: of every tribe of their fathers shall ye send a man, every one a ruler among them. . . .

17 And Moses sent them to spy out the land of Canaan, and said unto them, Get you up this way southward, and go up into the mountain:

18 And see the land, what it is; and the people that dwelleth therein, whether they be strong or weak, few or many;

19 And what the land is that they dwell in, whether it be good or bad; and what cities they be that they dwell in, whether in tents, or in strongholds;

20 And what the land is, whether it be fat or lean, whether there be wood therein, or not. And be ye of good courage, and bring of the fruit of the land. . . .

If you want to get off to a good start and enjoy early success in pioneering a new work, I highly recommend that you visit and "spy out" the country in which you are desiring to work.

See it firsthand, eat with the people there, and sleep in their homes. You need to walk through their villages and cities and attempt to identify with and understand them in every area of their lives. Listen to their dreams, desires, hopes, and fears.

1 CORINTHIANS 9:20-23

20 And unto the Jews I became as a Jew, that I might gain the Jews; to them that are under the law, as under the law, that I might gain them that are under the law;

21 To them that are without law, as without law, (being not without law to God, but under the law to Christ,) that I might gain them that are without law.

22 To the weak became I as weak, that I might gain the weak: I am made all things to all men, that I might by all means save some.

23 And this I do for the gospel's sake, that I might be partaker thereof with you.

When you visit the country to which you believe God is sending you, you will quickly find out whether or not you are called to that land. Many people have a very romantic idea about what it means to be a missionary. They are in love with the image, but the reality is quite different. There will be a lot of hard work, and you will no longer be in America. Everything takes longer to accomplish, and corruption and thievery are often rampant.

You will have to be wise as well as spiritually sensitive or you will be robbed blind. We have learned the hard way and God's way. We have seen many missionaries lose thousands of dollars as well as valuable equipment by not functioning in wisdom and listening to the Holy Ghost.

There are giants in the land that do not want you there. Poverty, religion, culture, traditions, rampant inflation, and racial prejudice are just some of the giants in the land. These are some of the realities that you will find in abundance on the mission field. Your attitude toward these challenges and obstacles will determine your success.

A visit to the country will bring a better understanding of what you will be up against, but it will also cause you to be better prepared and equipped to succeed and produce fruit for the Kingdom of God. When you can say with great boldness and confidence what Caleb said, "*. . . Let us go up at once, and possess it; for we are well able to overcome it*" (Num. 13:30), then you are probably called and ready to shake the kingdom of darkness by becoming a giant-killer!

4. **Vision and Strategy.**

   A. **Vision.** It is important that you understand your purpose and call to the mission field. A well-defined vision is necessary to keep you on track, because without it, your work will seem aimless, and you will have a difficult time judging whether you are reaching your goals and accomplishing your vision.

   B. **Strategy.** Just to say that you are going to preach the Gospel is to oversimplify a very complex procedure and will reveal a lack of planning. And planning is necessary in order to have long-term effectiveness and success. For example, *how* are you going to preach the Gospel? Through crusades? Seminars? Radio? Television? Bible schools? If you are going to hit the target, your aim has to be sure, so do not waste valuable resources just "trying something until it finally works."

   We wrote our vision down when we realized what we were called to do.

   HABAKKUK 2:2,3

   2 And the Lord answered me, and said, WRITE the vision, and make it plain upon tables, that he may RUN that READETH it.

   3 For the vision is yet for an appointed time, but at the end it shall speak, and not lie: though it tarry, wait for it; because it will surely come, it will not tarry.

   Notice that the Lord says to do three things: *write, run,* and *read.*

   Writing the vision down helps to establish it in your heart.

   Running with the vision is the direction and strategy you are to follow in accomplishing that vision.

Reading the vision helps you, as well as those who will work with you, to stay on course. It will help those who work with you catch hold of and understand what God is calling you to do.

C. **Goals.** In my opinion, goal-setting is essential in measuring progress and success as well as in helping determine your plan for expansion.

Make sure you set long- and short-term goals that are in focus and in line with what God has called you to accomplish for Him. When you reach your short-term goals, they will bring you closer to your long-range goals!

Setting goals will also help you plan ahead and will give the Holy Spirit an opportunity to reveal to you what you need to trust God for in the area of provision and spiritual needs.

JOHN 16:13

13 Howbeit when he, the Spirit of truth, is come, he will guide you into all truth: for he shall not speak of himself; but whatsoever he shall hear, that shall he speak: and he will shew you things to come.

It is better to begin to trust God now for things you will need in the future than to wish you had those things *yesterday*! Remember, keep your goals consistent with your vision and with the focus of your ministry.

5. **Develop a budget.**

A. **Spending.** As I shared earlier, try to keep all your expenses to a minimum until you are able to ascertain what your monthly support is going to be. In our situation, we were not sure what our monthly support was going to be. We had a general idea, but some of the churches that were supporting us did not tell us exactly how much they would be supporting us with.

However, after four to six months on the field, we did have an average amount per month that we could count on. This does not mean we did nothing for six months — we did plenty! We sacrificed some of our personal needs to accomplish what God brought us to Africa to do. Later, we had a little more financial leeway, and the "extras" that we needed personally became affordable.

B. **Budget considerations.** Some of the things you will have to keep in mind when developing a budget on the mission field are the costs of running and maintaining a vehicle, insurance, the price of food to feed your family, rent, and travel expenses.

Also, what types of supplies (literature, tracts, Bibles, and so forth) do you need to assist you in your work? Do not forget about water and electric bills. Check the price of gasoline. On the average, and depending on what country we are working in, we pay $3 - $5 a gallon. Careful research is needed in planning a budget for the mission field. The old saying "To be forewarned is to be forearmed" is a good piece of advice to remember.

You will also have expenses such as a newsletter, a phone or fax bill to the U.S., and possibly a salary or fee for someone to handle your finances and business affairs in the U.S.

During our first year on the mission field, we averaged between $700 and $1,000 a month in support. The house we were renting cost us $140 a month, which included water and electric payment. We spent about $100 a month on food, and our biggest ministry expense was buying fuel for traveling from country to country, preaching and teaching the Word of God.

As the ministry grew, so did the budget and the ability to accomplish more. Do not forget what the Word of God has to say: *"For who hath despised the day of small things? . . ."* (Zech. 4:10) and *". . .Well done, thou good and faithful servant: thou hast been faithful over a few things, I will make thee ruler over many things: enter thou into the joy of thy lord"* (Matt. 25:21).

6. Do the right thing!

A.   Integrity. When Jesus told the parable of the sower in Mark 4, He described a type of ground in verses 18 and 19: *"And these are they which are sown among thorns; such as hear the word, And the cares of this world, and the deceitfulness of riches, and the lusts of other things entering in, choke the word, and it becometh unfruitful."*

Guard your heart at all times, and do not allow the pressures of the ministry to cause you to compromise your integrity. I have watched other missionaries get thrown out of countries for breaking all kinds of laws trying to stay on the mission field. We knew one couple who worked in a nation under a tourist visa for two years, and the government finally caught up with them. They said, "No one is a tourist for two years" and expelled them from the country.

You may have to enter a country with a tourist visa, but start working right away on a work permit and resident visa. Obey the laws of the land. You are a guest in that country, and you represent the Lord Jesus Christ. As the saying goes, *whatever you compromise to keep, you will surely end up losing.*

While in that nation, make sure you keep your ministry legal. If it needs to be registered, do it and hire a good lawyer to advise you (he will be as important to you as your fax machine!).

Remember to ask lots of questions and find out from other ministries in the country what is required of you. Stay legal and walk in integrity and love. Your faith will bring you through all the difficult obstacles. Always remember God is *for* you and He has given you favor.

ACTS 2:47

47 Praising God, and having favour with all the people. And the Lord added to the church daily such as should be saved.

ACTS 7:10

10 And delivered him out of all his afflictions, and gave him favour and wisdom in the sight of Pharaoh king of Egypt; and he made him governor over Egypt and all his house.

If God is for you, who can be against you, so *do the right thing*!

7.   Ideas and Suggestions.

A.   Resources. Let me share with you a couple of helpful ideas to assist you in getting established: Purchase a good map of the nation in which you are planning to work. Study it and become familiar with the country. Know the cities, towns, and landmarks.

I would also recommend getting all the travel books you can find. They will provide you with a lot of valuable information. We found one that has saved us time and money and has given us a tremendous wealth of knowledge about the nations we are now reaching. The book is called *Africa on the Cheap*, published by Lonely Planet. It is a backpacker's guide to the countries of Africa and it lists places to stay, eat, and see.

I know this company has researched a lot of countries, so check it out; you might find this company very useful. Go to your local library and check out all the books you can about your destination country. Make sure you study and read the history. Also, look for travel videos and documentaries about your future home.

B. **Fellowship and relationships.** You will have the opportunity to meet some very interesting people on the mission field — missionaries, aid workers, and Americans on job contracts and on vacation, just to name a few. The local people will also greatly enrich your lives. The mission field can be a very lonely place if you let it.

I am encouraging you not to allow that to happen. Make friends even if you do not agree with them theologically. You will be blessed, and out of those relationships God will pour out wonderful blessings in the form of advice, help, and in numerous other areas.

We have watched missionaries who have kept to themselves suffer loneliness, depression, and trouble in their marriage because they would not reach out to people who might not believe exactly like they did. This is total stupidity and goes against what the Word of God teaches.

EPHESIANS 4:16

16 From whom the whole body fitly joined together and compacted by that which every joint supplieth, according to the effectual working in the measure of every part, maketh increase of the body unto the edifying of itself in love.

Work on building relationships with the established churches in the country. Missionaries who do not will suffer a great deal of unnecessary persecution. Remember, you are there to build the Kingdom of God, not your own kingdom.

C. **Establishing yourself.** I tell people all the time that where the will of God is for you, that is your home. Since God has called us to live and work in Africa, Africa is our home. You need to feel the same way about your destination country. You might have been born in America, but now you have a new home. See the will of God as your home, and it will help appropriate the grace of God in your life.

Most of the people in Africa were born there, and they did not have a choice about it. But my wife and I chose to obey God and come to Africa, so we are Africans *by choice*. You might say we're African-Americans!

D. **Prosperity.** I hope you pay careful attention to what I am about to share with you, as it will help you greatly. Many missionaries suffer from a poverty mentality that is often shoved on them by religion and the world. When people found out that we were going to the mission field, they unconsciously thought that my wife and I had taken a vow of poverty. They would tell us that we would be poor and never have anything nice.

This is a stronghold that the enemy sends to try and block out the truth in the Word of God. Stand firm against this lie.

God is your source. Do not ever forget that He wants nothing but the best for you in every area of your life. If you begin to accept the lie that a missionary is always poor, you will rob yourself and your family, and you will also discourage others from becoming missionaries.

People have tried to tell me that I should not dress so nice because no one will give me any money if I dress nice. They said that if I looked poor and needy, I could raise more money. But looking poor and needy only produces a guilt offering because you manipulated the people. This produces support that does not last, and when you are blessed, you have to hide it so people will not find out. Then you become a deceiver and a liar.

I know missionaries whom God has blessed with new cars, and when a visiting pastor from America comes over to see their missionary work, they hide the car so he will not see it. They are afraid that if he sees it, he might stop his support or think that the missionary has misused mission funds. I don't know about you, but to me, that is just dishonest!

A few years ago when our first child was born, another missionary told my wife that if she would go to a certain store and tell them she was a poor missionary, they would give her diapers almost free.

We could afford diapers, and we weren't going to lie or get something for free that we could afford. Besides, I am not going to confess over myself and my ministry that we are poor. We all know how powerful our words are.

In the last few years, there have been some books about missions that have advised people to support only missionaries who live at the level of the people they are ministering to in that country. I believe that this is very wrong for a few reasons.

First, it is unfair to penalize somebody for having faith and believing God or for being blessed by God. Again, this is poverty-thinking with the accompanying mentality that the God who is more than enough has become the God who is *barely* enough.

There is no recession in Heaven, and God is not repaving the streets of Heaven with copper because we spent all the gold. People who believe that missionaries should be poor become a respecter of persons, something that God is not.

Missionaries that accept a poverty mentality will "think poor" in every area of their lives. They will be spiritually poor, physically poor (lacking health), and materially poor. And they will produce poor results for God's Kingdom.

I have watched this firsthand. For many years, missionary children grew up thinking that God could only bless you if you lived in America. But look at what the Word of God says: *"If ye be willing and obedient, ye shall eat the good of the land"* (Isa. 1:19)! Psalm 112 also has something to say about the blessings of God:

PSALM 112:1-3

1 Praise ye the Lord. Blessed is the man that feareth the Lord, that delighteth greatly in his commandments.

2 His seed shall be mighty upon earth: the generation of the upright shall be blessed.

3 Wealth and riches shall be in his house: and his righteousness endureth for ever.

I hope you notice that there are no legal clauses attached to these verses of Scripture that exclude missionaries. Praise God! We can walk in all the blessings of God and not be ashamed, because the promises are all yes and amen in Christ (2 Cor. 1:20)!

I believe in giving, and I teach it everywhere we go. We have seen churches that were "dirt poor" begin to experience God's prosperity in their lives as they began to trust God in this area.

Do not forget the value of sowing and reaping. This article is not long enough for me to share with you all the wonderful things that God has provided for us through this avenue of blessing.

As a missionary, do not see yourself as someone others always have to give *to*. Begin to support other missionaries and other ministries. Some of the best ground we have ever sown into is RHEMA, and our support grows constantly because of this very fact.

One last thing on this subject that you need to remember is the fact that when Jesus taught on the subject of prosperity, He also said that persecution will always follow.

MARK 10:29,30

29 And Jesus answered and said, Verily I say unto you, There is no man that hath left house, or brethren, or sisters, or father, or mother, or wife, or children, or lands, for my sake, and the gospel's,

30 But he shall receive an hundredfold now in this time, houses, and brethren, and sisters, and mothers, and children, and lands, with persecutions; and in the world to come eternal life.

If you have not already noticed by now, some of that persecution will come from your own spiritual family, and that can hurt the most. But do not forget what Jesus said to do to those that persecute you.

MATTHEW 5:11,12,44,45

11 Blessed are ye, when men shall revile you, and persecute you, and shall say all manner of evil against you falsely, for my sake.

12 Rejoice, and be exceeding glad: for great is your reward in heaven: for so persecuted they the prophets which were before you. . . .

44 But I say unto you, Love your enemies, bless them that curse you, do good to them that hate you, and pray for them which despitefully use you, and persecute you;

45 That ye may be the children of your Father which is in heaven: for he maketh his sun to rise on the evil and on the good, and sendeth rain on the just and on the unjust.

When you pray for those who persecute you, you will help them out of their spiritual blindness and guard your own heart from feelings of bitterness and anger that will hinder you.

Do not allow public opinion to determine your economic status. The blessings of God will overtake you in a wonderful way because God is your source. People will never rise above the level of those who are bringing them truth. The example you set will inspire and motivate people not to limit God in their lives (Ps. 78:40-42).

8. **The Missionary's Family.**

   A. **Priorities.** One of the greatest stories I have ever heard on the mission field was from the son of a missionary. This son was in his forties and had taken over his father's work. He shared with me that when they first moved to Africa, he was just a child, and they were in a place that was very hot and humid during most of the year. The first thing that his father did for his family was to build a pool.

   It took the father an entire month of backbreaking labor to see the project through. But when it was finished, his father would come home every afternoon, and they would all go and take a swim and be refreshed together.

   This second-generation missionary told me that by his father building that pool, he let his family know how very important they were and that they came first in his life.

   Do not make your family suffer for the work of the ministry. They did not choose to be missionaries; *you* did. Do your best to see that they are not neglected. Spend quality time with them. Let them know that next to Jesus, they are more important than anything, including your work.

   If you do this, you will not lose your children, and they will not grow up thinking that God stole their daddy away from them. The Scripture says, *"But if any provide not for his own, and specially for those of his own house, he hath denied the faith, and is worse than an infidel"* (1 Tim. 5:8).

   We have seen some very sad situations arise because the father neglected his responsibility in caring and providing for his family. Divorce, marital infidelity, and rebellious children are all consequences of some form of neglect. There have been times when I felt it necessary to rearrange my schedule so that I could spend time with my family.

   We take regular vacations together and do fun things all the time. My wife and children know how important they are to me. A happy and contented family will be a source of success and confidence when the missionary has to be away from his family. While you are ministering life to others, do not forget your very own family.

9. **Raising Financial Support (the Sacred Cow).**

   A. **Stay in faith.** When I returned from my first mission trip, I knew that God had called me. I knew what I was to do, but I had no idea how to go about financing this work. When I spoke with other missionaries and asked them how to go about raising support, most of them were very tight-lipped and were not very helpful. Actually, from talking with them, you'd get the impression they were guarding the Colonel's secret recipe for fried chicken!

   So I had to rely on the Holy Spirit to show me what to do. Let me share something with you that I have learned over the years: Do not let monthly support become your sacred cow! Too many missionaries see monthly support as their source. But God is your source and will always be your source. Remember that and you will stay on track.

We have had times when our monthly support seemed to just dry up within weeks. One particular time, we were in the country of Mozambique holding crusades when our support just ceased to come in. But the Lord provided for us supernaturally in Mozambique, and we just carried on our work and saw more than 250,000 people saved!

Monthly support is a necessity for you to accomplish your work on the foreign field. So begin now to believe God for supporters and partners to get behind what God has called you to do.

B. **Presentation.** It is important that you present and communicate what you are going to do on the mission field in a very clear way and in the shortest amount of time possible. Put together a brochure and newsletter sharing the vision and accomplishments of your ministry.

Pictures are important, so get a large scrapbook and fill it with pictures that show your work in your nation and the culture and scenery of the country. Video is also a very useful tool in sharing your vision. Bring back artifacts and curios that help as conversation stimulators.

Remember, a sloppy presentation will reflect poorly on you and cause a loss of confidence in those looking to invest into your mission work. Put together your presentation with excellence, and people will know and see that you are committed to giving God your best on the mission field.

When you are given the opportunity to share before a church, do not beg for money or try and make the church feel guilty because they are blessed. Manipulation will backfire on you every time. There are many reasons why America is so blessed, so do not try to make people feel guilty about it.

Excitement and enthusiasm will reveal the fire that God has put in your heart for the nation He has called you to reach. If that church does not have a missions vision, and a lot of churches don't, this is your opportunity to turn that around by showing them the great need around the world! Show them how ripe the harvest is in your nation. People generally want to invest in something that will advance the Kingdom of God.

During your time of ministry to that church, do not just sell your vision, but put a deposit of truth into that congregation. If you will be concerned about being a blessing to that church and assisting in their growth, they will in turn want to assist you in yours.

When I visit a church for the first time, I will take some time in the beginning of my ministering to give the congregation an overview of what we are about and what great victories we have seen on the mission field.

During my preaching, I will include stories from the field that relate to my message. Remember, you are anointed to preach the Word, not to raise money. Faith and obedience will bring in your financial needs. Remember, *"If ye be willing and obedient, ye shall eat the good of the land"* (Isa. 1:19).

Let the pastor know that your goal is to raise monthly support. You will be amazed at how many pastors do not know a missionary needs monthly support. One of your responsibilities is to educate people. Ignorance and "fables" surround the mystique of a missionary. Bring them into the light of truth and reality.

C. **Supporters and partners.** These are the people that God is raising up on your behalf to finance the work He has called you to do for Him. They can be individuals as well as churches. Together, you will see great victories. They not only will give to you financially, but they will hold you up in prayer.

You are probably wanting to know where to find these people! You will find them everywhere. Some will be family members and others will be friends and acquaintances. Even businessmen who find out what you are doing will seek you out to support you.

Take every opportunity that comes your way to share your calling and vision with people, whether it is people in the Rotary Clubs, Lions Clubs, gardening clubs, Bible studies, or church meetings. In our first few years, 50 percent of our support came from individuals. As we have grown, that has gone down to about 20 percent, but our church support has increased greatly. I am telling you this so you won't concentrate exclusively on churches. Broaden your understanding and do not limit God.

When you are starting out, not many people will know you or have heard about you. They will say some very cruel things to you to sometimes try and discourage you or to make you feel that you are missing God. Most of those types of comments are out of pure ignorance and lack of understanding.

When my wife and I were traveling and sharing about our work and vision, people would say things like, "We support *home* missions. There are a lot of people here in the States who haven't heard." Or they would say, "We support So-and-so, and he's getting everybody saved in Africa, so you are just wasting your time!" or "We only believe in supporting nationals because they can do more for less."

This can be very discouraging to hear, but do not lose heart just because a lot of people have very confused opinions about the realities of missions. Do not let ignorant and uninformed opinions deter you from your goal.

Use your time wisely and visit as many pastors and churches as possible. This may sound easy, but it will take a bit of work on your part. Remember, Jesus said, "Seek, and you shall find"! Your partners are out there. You will have to find them.

Contact as many pastors as you can in your area and try and visit with them. If you can, it is best to speak to their church congregation, but that is not necessary on the first contact and probably will not happen since they do not know who you are.

Many times, sitting in the pastors' office or having lunch with them opens up an opportunity to return and share with their church what you are doing. Sharing your pictures and stories will help them see their need to become involved.

Sometimes they will say that at the present time, they are already committed in their budget but that they will be praying for you. You may hear back from them later that their budget has increased and that they are picking you up for support! Many times pastors could not help us with monthly support, but before I left they handed me a check to bless our work.

Do not make the mistake of trying to contact only RHEMA pastors for support. I have contacted churches that do not believe exactly the way we do, but they have a heart to reach the world with the Gospel, and they did not know any missionaries until I contacted them. We have Baptist, Presbyterian, Assemblies of God, and Church of God churches that support our work. Some of these churches have incredible resources to sow into missions, but they are never approached by missionaries.

When you are traveling to a new area, open the phone book and begin to call the churches in that area. Ask the pastor if you may come by and share with him about your work on the mission field. Explain to him very politely that you are raising support and that you are excited about what God is doing in your land. Ask if he would like to hear about it. The worst thing that can happen to you is that he may say he is not interested. Call someone else.

Before most pastors support a missionary, they want to get to know the missionary and the missionary's family. It is vitally important that you understand that the Kingdom of God is built on relationships.

1 THESSALONIANS 5:12

12 And we beseech you, brethren, to know them which labour among you. . . .

Partners and supporters of your work should be more than anonymous givers. They are part of your family. In a crisis, they will be there to pull you out — through their prayers and finances. Build relationships with pastors and churches, and as they grow, so will their support for your work.

Take time to visit conferences and seminars that will help put you in contact with other pastors. These meetings provide a very non-threatening atmosphere to meet people who will ask you what you do. This will bring you many opportunities to share about your work.

Some of the pastors you visit may not hook up with you right away. Many will take a "wait and see" approach toward you and your work. The reason for this is that so many missionaries quit after about a year, and the churches feel let down, so they begin to look for those missionaries who are established and who have roots. You will notice that the longer you are on the field, the easier it is to increase your monthly support.

One final thought on this subject is to begin now to believe God for those partners you need. Here is a good scripture to begin to stand on: *"A man's gift maketh room for him, and bringeth him before great men"* (Prov. 18:16).

You will need what this scripture promises, both here in America *and* on the mission field. I believe all pastors are great men, and great men are always generous, helpful, and supportive. God will bring pastors like Meshach, Shadrach and Abednego across your path to stand with you and not allow you to bend your knee to any form of compromise. They will encourage you to stand firm in faith not wavering.

D. **Newsletters.** Pastors have shared with me that one of the things they do *not* like is not hearing regularly from the missionary they are supporting. Your most valuable asset in communicating your ministry's successes, trials, and needs is your newsletter.

Your newsletter is the equivalent of a church's offering plate. You are not using it to beg for money but to give people an opportunity to bless you with an offering. Many times your newsletter will remind your partners that they are supporting you. "Out of sight, out of mind" is a real problem for missionaries, and the newsletter acts as a pleasant reminder for supporters to pray and to give.

The content of your newsletter should tell what you are doing on the field. It should share your triumphs and good reports as well as some of the struggles so your friends and supporters can pray for you. If at all possible, try to include pictures, because pictures speak very loudly what you are trying to share in print.

Do not turn your newsletter into a teaching format. I know some missionaries who do that, and they are constantly struggling to get support. People want to know what you are doing, and that is why they are investing in you. Your newsletter is a major way to stay accountable to the people who are supporting you.

10. Business.

A. Incorporation. When we first started out, we were under our home church's incorporation. They were very supportive in the beginning, but as our work began to grow, they were not able to keep up with all of our stateside needs. Problems began to arise, and our monthly support was not being collected at the post office as quickly as it should have been and deposited in our bank. This created many very aggravating problems for us.

Our pastor had never had the opportunity to visit us on the foreign field, so he had no idea of the cost of living there. There is an opinion in America that it is cheaper to live in third-world countries than it is in America. In my travels and conversations with other missionaries, I have found that this is not true. Our pastor also had this opinion and would constantly question certain ministry expenses. This hindered us in the purchase of much-needed equipment and even in our living expenses.

If I had it to do over again, I would have hooked up with a missions service agency. There are some excellent ones. So do your research and ask other missionaries how they feel about the service they are receiving. Service agencies understand the needs of a missionary much better than most churches. Most of these agencies will charge about 10 percent of your monthly support as a service fee, and that is not excessive compared to all that they will provide for you.

For example, if your monthly income or budget is $1,500 a month, service agencies will charge $150 for their services. This usually includes picking up your mail and depositing monies into your bank account, receipting all your donors, and sending out a newsletter. You will usually have to pay postage, and there are many other services that they will perform for you for a nominal charge. This is the best way to go if you are just starting out.

As you grow, it will be imperative that you set up your own office. When your support grows to the point that the 10 percent you are paying an agency can pay for a full-time office person whose full focus is on your ministry, take that step and never look back, because it will be one of the best decisions you can make.

Doing that will mean that you will have to form your own incorporation. Every state has different requirements, so get a good lawyer that specializes in this field. I know that some people try to do it on their own to save a lawyer's fee. But over the years I have heard many horror stories and have seen ministries get into serious legal trouble trying to save a buck. Remember, we serve El Shaddai, not "El Cheapo." Our God can afford a good lawyer!

When choosing board members, we only have people on our board who have visited us and have worked with us on the mission field. This way, they have an intimate knowledge about our work, the things we deal with, and the conditions. They understand our economy and our personal needs, and this is important. Most importantly, they are in agreement with our vision. By working with us, they have seen firsthand as the vision *has been* and *is being* accomplished.

Take my advice: A board member will be able to serve you to a higher degree if he has visited and worked with you on the mission field.

11. **Visiting Home and Itinerating.**

A. **Rest and relaxation.** It is very important that you go home to the States or your native country for rest and relaxation. Too many missionaries have burned-out because they did not take time to rest. Even God rested, and we see in the Gospels that Jesus took His disciples away for a rest (Mark 6:31,32).

Getting away from the daily work of the ministry from time to time will get you recharged and refocused. There have been times while I was laying on the beach soaking up some sunshine that God began to show me new direction for our work! He even showed me some things that I needed to deal with that I had not noticed while I was in the middle of it. Rest is not only important for you, but your family will probably need as much or even more rest than you will.

B. **Itinerating.** It is important during your time in the States that you go back to the churches that support you to share with them your progress and to visit new churches.

When we go home to the States, we have many different goals to accomplish, two of which are to increase our monthly support and to raise additional funding to cover special projects such as purchasing vehicles, land, or constructing a building. All of these are outside the scope of our monthly support.

How often a missionary comes home depends on many things. The cost of the return is a major consideration, and the purpose of the visit is another. The independent missionary will come home more often because he is solely responsible to raise his support, not having a denomination behind him to finance his programs.

We have been away as long as two years before we visited home in the States, and some years we were in the States twice, so it varies with the needs and the types of mission work.

In the early years of our work, when we would go home for a visit, we stayed sometimes for three months itinerating. We are not able to do that any longer because we have grown, and our schedule is too full in Africa. With growth comes employees and many other responsibilities, so now we go home for a shorter period, sometimes twice a year.

As a rule, when we do go back for a visit, we try to time it with a major event at RHEMA, such as Winter Bible Seminar or Campmeeting. These are all times of great refreshing for us and an important way for us to stay hooked up with our spiritual roots. Your time home should be used wisely and be productive both for you and your ministry.

12. **Keep yourself built up.**

A. **Stay "plugged in."** One of the biggest reasons for missionaries failing in their work is that they do not make a conscious effort to keep themselves in top spiritual condition. In the beginning of this chapter, I said that it was important for you to know who you are as a son of God, and that knowledge comes two ways: By study and by your intimacy with God.

With all the discipling you will be doing, do not lose sight that you are also a disciple and that you need to grow in wisdom and knowledge.

I have a number of friends who send me good books and tapes. I have a circle of friends on the mission field to whom I can go for fellowship, advice, and counsel. I have relationships with pastors in the States whom I can call day or night (collect!) to talk and pray with me. Many times, they call me just to let me know they are praying for us.

When I am back in America, I always attend some meeting to be fed the Word of God.

DANIEL 11:32

32 . . .but the people that do know their God shall be strong, and do exploits.

Follow this advice and you will *pioneer in power*!

Chapter 3

Answering the Call to the Nations

By Jim ('80) and Brenda (Tate) Puhr ('79 '80)

Jim and Brenda Puhr are both graduates of RHEMA Bible Training Center. They have been missionaries for more than 13 years. In 1982 they moved to Costa Rica, Central America, where they served for six years. Along with several others, the Puhrs also helped establish Calvary International, a missions agency based in Jacksonville, Florida, that now has more than 200 missionaries in 16 nations.

For the past three years, Jim and Brenda have served in Moscow, Russia, where they've helped start a Bible school. The Puhrs also travel throughout Russia, helping local churches.

The Puhrs have three children: Nathan, age 11; Ryan, age 8; and Alexandra, age 1.

We'll never forget the day we first arrived in Costa Rica, Central America. It was January 3, 1982 — a day that we had prayed about, dreamed about, and a day that we sometimes wondered if we'd ever see. It was our first day as foreign missionaries.

It's been more than 13 years since that day. Since that time we have traveled to more than a dozen countries, helping to start several Bible schools. We've lived in four of those countries and have seen tens of thousands of people come to Christ.

We still remember clearly the many questions we had when we first made the decision to become missionaries (it was only a year and a half before we actually left for the foreign field). They were questions that most missionaries have when deciding to go on the field: the "how," "who," "what," "when," and "where" questions — questions such as, "How will we raise the money to go? Who will support us? Where exactly are we supposed to go? What about the language barrier? What will we do when we get there?" The questions go on and on.

Although we are sharing our thoughts and ideas on missions, not enough can be said about all the *w-o-r-k* that is involved in missions ministry. From the very start — from our first step of planning — to this very day, *the work has never stopped*! And it's the practical everyday things that are sometimes the most challenging.

We would like to share two "stages" to becoming a successful missionary. We have experienced these stages firsthand. The things discussed in these two stages are the areas we are most asked about by those who are praying about answering the missionary call. Each of these stages has its own challenges and victories. The two stages are what we call "The Decision and Preparation Stage" and "The First Year on the Field Stage."

Stage 1: Decision and Preparation

The first stage to becoming a successful missionary is often the stage most people who are called to be missionaries can't get past. This stage consists of the practical step-by-step process of getting to the field.

Historically, most people who wanted to be missionaries just went through their own denomination or other missions organization that their church was affiliated with. But since Charismatic churches are independent and the Charismatic Movement a relatively new movement, there are few ties to missions organizations. Therefore, Charismatics who are called to be missionaries often do not know where to turn to get step-by-step advice on how to get to the field.

Here's what we did:

Brenda and I had very different backgrounds. She is from Lakeland, Florida, and grew up as a Southern Baptist. Even her grandfather has been a Southern Baptist minister for more than 50 years. She attended RHEMA Bible Training Center with her parents in 1978 when she was 18 years old.

I am from Boulder, Colorado, and grew up in a strong Catholic family. I had no desire to be in the ministry. I received Christ as a senior in high school — the first time I'd heard the Gospel. It was at a Crusade in Loveland, Colorado. In 1979 I attended RHEMA with several friends from what was then my home church, Calvary Temple, in Denver, Colorado.

It was while studying at RHEMA that I first felt that one day I would be a missionary. After Brenda and I met at RHEMA, one of the first things we talked about when we started to date was what we felt God's plans were for each of our lives. We both felt that we would be foreign missionaries.

After graduating from RHEMA in 1980, we moved to Gainesville, Florida, and got married. We began to serve as Children's Church ministers at a small new church there. We didn't receive a salary from the church, but we were both happy just to be ministering.

Determine God's Will for *Your* Life

Immediately after graduating from RHEMA, we had begun telling people that we were going to the mission field. Often, people didn't take us seriously, or they tried to discourage us. They would say that there was plenty of work to do in the United States, so why should we go overseas to minister.

We have always sought the will of the Lord for our lives, and we believe that God puts the desire in people's hearts to become missionaries. When you know the will of the Lord for your life, you can put your faith in what He has put in your heart. Then when the tests and challenges come, you will have the faith to go through them.

Agreement in Marriage

Of course, it is essential that a husband and wife be in complete agreement that being missionaries is the will of God for their lives. Agreement is essential before you get on an airplane and go to a foreign country to live! Why? Because when you step out to do God's will, you can be assured that the enemy will tell you time and time again that you're not in the will of God.

For us, after being discouraged by several missions organizations who said we didn't qualify for various reasons, we called a missionary who had been a guest speaker in one of our classes while we were attending RHEMA. He was living in Ciudad Victoria, Mexico, at that time.

After we contacted him, he suggested that we come down to Mexico for a week to see if we were really serious about becoming missionaries. He said that spending a week in a foreign country, where they eat different foods, speak a different language, and have a different culture, can sometimes help confirm the calling on a person's life.

So we packed our little Chevy and drove to Ciudad Victoria! I'll never forget the day — November 8, 1981 — we crossed from Brownsville, Texas, to Matamoros, Mexico. That day God put a supernatural love in our hearts for the Latin people. It was also our first wedding anniversary.

Spending that week there accomplished three distinct things in our lives:

First, it confirmed in our hearts that God had called us to be missionaries!

Second, it gave us direction as to what our next step should be. If we were going to be missionaries to Latin America, we needed to learn Spanish. Therefore, we decided we would go to a Spanish language school designed specifically for missionaries. The one we chose was located in San Jose, Costa Rica.

Third, that week in Mexico armed us with information concerning a budget as well as several simple steps on how to raise the needed financial support. We received answers to many questions we had about the practical aspects of missionary life, such as: newsletters, mailing lists, legal aspects, and the timing as to when to leave for the field.

We encourage anyone who is thinking about becoming a foreign missionary and has never been out of the United States on a missions trip, to take a trip to a mission field or to the country where he or she has a heart to work. The dollars spent on this trip are usually well worth the investment. For us, the trip to Mexico was life-changing.

We even encourage those who want to come help us in Russia, where we are now serving, to visit first before making the decision to move here. If the people are married, we ask both husbands and wives to visit.

If prospective missionaries have traveled overseas a lot, it may not be necessary for them to make another trip, as they probably have most of their questions answered already.

After You Determine God's Will, Be Determined to Fulfill It!

I well remember back in late 1981, just weeks before we were to leave for Costa Rica, Brenda began to have doubts as to whether we were doing the right thing. The reason she began to doubt was that things weren't going the way we thought they should be going. We had the misconception that since we were "in God's will," everything would just "come together."

Instead, everything began to fall apart! Brenda was in a car accident (she wasn't hurt), the house that we owned at the time didn't sell, our support wasn't coming in like we thought it would, and our friends and family were discouraging us from going overseas.

As soon as she began to doubt, we sat down and talked about the things that God had put in our hearts, and she was able to get back in faith. Since that time, we have never doubted what God's will was for our lives. As I said, it is absolutely essential that the question of whether it's God's will for you to be a missionary be answered *before* you go to the foreign field, because the enemy will continually challenge you on it.

Every time something went wrong or when something didn't go the way we thought it should go, we were able to rest on our faith that we knew we were in the will of God.

Be Diligent in Your Business Affairs

In preparing to go to the field, don't leave the devil any open doors through which he can enter once you get overseas. In other words, oftentimes, because of our zeal to get to the field, we fail to fully take care of the practical aspects of both personal and ministry issues. Some of these issues might include things such as getting insurance, deciding whether to sell or rent your house, taking care of debt that you might have, and so forth.

We realized a long time ago that while, yes, it's hard to get to the mission field, it's harder still to stay there! We could probably name at least a dozen missionaries who have had to leave the mission field or who were greatly impaired in their mission work because they didn't take care of some of these things before they left America.

For example, we've witnessed some missionaries renting out their houses in America while they were overseas, and they lost money because the renters became delinquent in paying their rent. The situations looked "perfect" at first, yet a few months later, the renters would suddenly move or leave because they couldn't pay the rent. Then the missionaries had to use a fairly large percentage of their missionary support to make their house payments. More often than not, those missionaries were off the field within a year.

Getting Stateside Help

Of course, one of the most important aspects of going to the mission field is deciding who will be taking care of your finances. The person who handles the stateside affairs is the missionary's lifeline.

The handling of finances is usually done one of three different ways: through a missions organization, a local church, or through the missionary's own non-profit ministry.

There are pros and cons to each of these three means of handling a ministry's business affairs. Each missionary has to seek God as to which means would be best in his or her situation. We have seen all three ways work well, and we've also seen them work disastrously!

The majority of all missionaries around the world go out on the field through missions organizations such as Campus Crusade, Wycliffe, Youth With a Mission, or denominations such as the Assemblies of God.

The advantage of going through a missions organization is that these organizations usually have a proven track record and are strong in administration. The disadvantages are that the organizations can sometimes be confining and many times have heavy administrative expenses. Oftentimes, the expenses are justifiable, incorporating such things as health and life insurance and retirement plans.

The missions organization that we're a part of has not been without its own challenges. It is important to understand up front that there is no perfect ministry or organization.

Our missions organization, Calvary International, has about 200 missionaries serving in about 16 countries. Calvary International charges a 10-percent service fee from the offerings that come through the ministry. The organization provides field oversight and helps people get to the field through 10 days of training in our international offices in Florida.

The training includes everything from support development and newsletters to how to obtain insurance overseas and getting long-term visas to the country where a person plans to serve. Essentially, all the practical aspects of getting to the field and being a success there are taught in these sessions.

As with most Charismatic missions agencies, we have had our challenges as to what role to play in the missionary's life once he or she arrives on the field. Some missionaries want a lot of oversight and direction, while others just want to use the organization as a way to get to the field. Once they arrive, they want to be on their own without the direct input of the home office.

Another way many missionaries take care of their finances and administrative needs is directly through their home church. We've seen this work excellently, but more often, we've seen it become frustrating for the missionary. Of course, the advantage of working through your church is the hands-on role the church plays in your life. For example, they see firsthand how much support you get. But problems can occur when the church changes pastors or secretaries.

Also, it needs to be understood that the pastor and secretary are overseeing or are involved in at least a half dozen other areas of the church and not just in missions work. Working through your church works well when the church has its own department and staff that only handle missions work.

Yet still another way that missionaries handle the financial and administrative aspects of missions is to set up their own ministry. That way they, too, have control of whatever happens. This can prove to be expensive and is also usually very dependent upon one or two people — oftentimes volunteers back home. We have never opted to use this means, so we cannot say much about it.

Raising Financial Support

One of the most challenging and sometimes frightening things for those thinking about becoming missionaries is the whole idea of "fund-raising." Maybe it's because we have seen so many bad examples of ministers "begging" for money, and we don't want to be seen in the same light. Or maybe we feel deep down that it's a compromise to ask for support when we're supposed to "just believe God to meet our needs."

Yet another principle reason for disliking this aspect of missionary life is our culture, which goes against asking people for money. It simply goes against our pride to ask other people for money.

Whatever the reason, this is one of the biggest obstacles to people going overseas to be missionaries. When we talk to those praying about becoming missionaries, we advise them not to let the question of finances be the deciding factor as to whether or not to proceed. As we said before, your motivation should be "What is the will of God for my life?" If God's will is for you to be a missionary, then you need to run with that vision and do whatever it takes to fulfill His will for your life!

One of the keys to successful support development is your attitude. We personally view support development as just as much a part of our ministry as working with pastors in Russia or helping set up a Bible school.

An obstacle that many prospective missionaries have is the attitude, "When I raise my support and get to the mission field, *then* I will begin my ministry." They see the support development aspect of missions as a necessary evil — something that they *have* to do. This attitude comes across to others; therefore, the process of raising support becomes something the missionaries struggle through.

We encourage those who feel called to missions to look at support development as ministry to the Body of Christ! It can serve the purpose of increasing believers' vision for missions and of developing relationships with pastors and your support team — those who will pray for you. These relationships will help you tremendously as you fulfill God's will for you life.

Yet another problem that missionaries frequently have is one that they themselves have caused. It's an attitude of "just getting by financially."

When prospective missionaries are asked how much money they need to live on a certain foreign field, we often hear them respond, "We can get by on…," which is usually much less than they really need to do what they feel God has called them to do.

As a result of that "just getting by" attitude, every area of their ministry suffers. Their family suffers because their children don't get the practical things or the education they need. The wife doesn't get her washing machine or even nice clothes. Quite often these "little things" cause problems in the home and force the missionary off the field.

As we said, the deciding factor in fulfilling God's call and in the success of raising your support should not be your ability to raise support but rather "What is the will of God for my life?" If God's will is that you be a foreign missionary, then He will provide the means to fulfill it.

We believe strongly that faith begins where the will of God is known. But at the same time, faith always involves action or *w-o-r-k*. In other words, things won't "just happen" for you just because you're in the will of God. You do have to do your part in raising support.

For example, more than 98 percent of all missionaries on the field today are supported by churches and individuals. The other two percent are supported through their own sources such as savings or another source of income.

If you become a part of a missions organization, that organization will usually teach you about ethical ways to raise support.

Another option for learning support development is to contact a missions organization that teaches support development seminars for their missionaries. Ask them if you may attend one of their seminars (if you are married, your spouse should attend also).

Stage 2: The First Year on the Field

Quite often new missionaries to any field are very idealistic. They have been dreaming about being a missionary, and when they finally arrive on the field they think they can win the whole city in the first year.

This brings to mind the story of the new missionary arriving in Mexico City (the largest city in the world) and asking a veteran missionary who had been there for more than 30 years why he hadn't won the city to Christ yet. The wise veteran didn't want to quench the zeal of the new missionary, so he decided to help channel that energy in reaching the city. The new missionary found out soon enough that winning a city is a lot easier said than done!

Don't Neglect Valuable Preparation Time
Once You're on the Field

An overseas missionary needs to plan according to the length of time he plans to stay overseas. When Brenda and I first went to Costa Rica, we planned to study the language for the first eight months we were there. We viewed this time spent learning the language as something just as important as preaching. After six months of language school, I began to minister in Spanish. After a couple of years, I even began to interpret for people coming to the field to visit.

When we moved to Russia we spent the first three months learning the language even though we had only planned to live in Russia one year. Learning Russian was quite a bit harder than learning Spanish. But even with three months of classes, we were able to communicate with the pastors. And now we are very happy that we took the time to learn the basics of Russian, as our time here has "broadened" to three years!

We feel that during the first year on the field, the new missionary should concentrate on learning the language and culture and on settling his family in their new environment. Oftentimes, missionaries feel pressure to perform because of expectations from their home churches, people that support them, or themselves (missionaries often put pressure on themselves to prove that they are really supposed to be there).

In all the years that we've been involved with missions, we've seen very few lazy missionaries, but we have seen many who probably overwork, over-preach, and who are always busy. I remember one year when we lived in Costa Rica, I preached about 175 times. This sounds great, but the problem was my family suffered, the quality of my message wasn't that good, and my motives for doing that weren't always right. Also, my time spent with the Lord was not what it should have been.

Get God's Plan for Your Harvest Field

While we lived in Costa Rica, we were in the midst of a revival. The number of churches in the nation had grown from 700 to more than 2,000 in a period of just a few years.

Our strategy was to help start a Bible training center (Cristo al Mundo) to help train the pastors and many leaders that had just recently come to Christ. During that time more than 1,000 students graduated from the one-year school.

In Russia our strategy is just a little different. In 1989 when we first considered it as a field for ministry, the Iron Curtain had just come down, and the doors of opportunity to the Soviet Union were beginning to open. We had heard of the things that Jim Kaseman Ministries, Terry Law Ministries, and many other ministries had been doing during the many years when it was difficult to minister in the Soviet Union.

Two of Calvary International's board members visited the Soviet Union in late 1989, and they encouraged the leaders of Calvary International to explore the possibility of working there.

We took a trip to the Soviet Union in April 1990 and decided to open a Bible school there. We sent several families and singles to the Soviet Union, and in January 1991 opened the school with 121 students. They had come from the Ukraine, Estonia, Soviet Georgia, Uzbekistan, Siberia, and from throughout the entire Soviet Union.

Since that time, more than 450 students have graduated, and we continue to have the school here in Moscow. More than 100 churches have been started by the graduates of the Bible school.

Our strategy in Russia has been to help reach out to the large number of new converts and get them established in churches. We have networked with many other organizations that are also working here, including: CBN, Teen Mania Ministries, Terry Law Ministries, and Campus Crusade for Christ.

Many fields around the world are like Costa Rica and Russia, where there are great harvests. Yet in many countries, such as those in western Europe, the people aren't nearly as responsive to the Gospel. In each country we work in, we develop a unique strategy for that nation. Each country's ground for reaping a harvest is different. For example, what works in eastern Europe may not work in western Europe.

The key is to have a strategy. If you have a vision and a plan, you can fulfill your ministry. If you lose that vision, you will become frustrated and lose sight of your goal.

Suggestions for Prospective Missionaries

1. Don't be quick to judge other missionaries or ministries in the country that you are working in. Quite often your attitude toward them will change after a few months.

2. Don't ever criticize or listen to people criticize churches, pastors, other missionaries, or ministries. Oftentimes doing this will "come back to hurt you." Also, quite often the things you hear are not true, but the devil tries to sow discord everywhere.

3. Don't be quick to leave the people or ministry you work with because of problems. Oftentimes new missionaries have an idealistic view of how people should work together and get along. Try to work things out and look to see if the problem possibly lies with you and your attitude.

4. Keep your priorities in line: God first, family second, and ministry third. The more these three areas of your life get out of order and the longer they *stay* out of order, the more damage it will cause.

5. Try to continually educate yourself. Read and study all you can about your field and your areas of ministry. The more information you have, the more effective you will be.

6. Develop people skills. This is an area that is probably one of the most important but least studied by people going into the ministry. Read books to help you understand people's personality traits. There are several ministries that deal specifically with this area. They provide tapes and books that can be of great help.

7. Do not develop a superiority attitude. It's easy for missionaries to think that they have made a greater sacrifice than other Christians because they have "left all" to serve the Lord. And oftentimes they want to let pastors and friends know in subtle ways all that they have given up. This sometimes comes across that the missionary thinks he or she is "special." This attitude turns people off, not only toward the individual, but toward missionaries in general.

8. Do not compare yourself with other missionaries. Do not compare your results with the results of other missionaries. Be concerned about what God has called *you* to do. The Apostle Paul said in Corinthians that he who compares himself with another is not wise (2 Cor. 10:12).

9. Take the time to pray.

10. Develop long-term goals. Don't just plan for next week or next year. Make goals concerning setting up a retirement account or setting aside finances for your children's college tuition.

Conclusion

As a final thought to those thinking about becoming missionaries or even to those who are now serving around the world: Only eternity will tell of all the lives that will be and have been changed because of your decision concerning being a missionary.

The devil does everything he can to keep us from fulfilling God's will for our lives. So armed with that knowledge, never give up! Don't ever give up!

Chapter 4

Recognizing and Pursuing the Missionary Call

By Joe Purcell ('87 '88)

Joe and Mary Purcell are missionaries to far northeastern Siberia in a region of Russia known as Chukotka, which is situated directly across the Bering Sea from Alaska. They live in the city of Provideniya with their four children: Joe, age 11; Peter, age 9; John, age 7; and Katie, age 4.

Joe graduated from RHEMA Bible Training Center in 1988. Prior to entering the ministry full time in 1989, he practiced law for 11 years. Before moving to Russia, Joe was involved in a missionary-evangelist ministry to the Alaskan bush. He began traveling to Provideniya in March 1991. Since September 1992, the Purcells have lived in Provideniya, where they have established a church and are developing a missionary outreach team to bring the full Gospel to this unevangelized part of the world.

If you never have been a missionary on the foreign field and you sense that God may be calling you to that ministry, you no doubt have many questions. "Am I really called to be a missionary? How shall I prepare myself? How do I raise support? Should I incorporate? What about our children?"

In short, you want to know how to get started. There is a way!

The Missionary Call

The primary way you know you are called to missions *in particular* is the same way you know you are called to the ministry *in general*: *by the inward witness of the Holy Spirit!*

Your call may be spectacular; it may be subtle. In either event, you will know by the inward witness of the Spirit in your spirit. Much has been written already on that subject, and it is not my intention to reiterate here what others have expressed better elsewhere. Instead, I want to mention a few things that helped me to recognize and follow the leading of the Lord in my own life.

The grace of God upon your life is direction. One way to discover that grace is to begin ministering in your local church in any capacity the pastor desires. Your gifts and abilities will begin to surface. The gift of God in you will be nurtured and will begin to manifest itself. That gift of God in you is direction!

The desires that God places in your heart are also direction. It took me a long time to realize that. I grew up in a denomination which taught that whatever you truly desire in life is what God will require you to forego. What nonsense! If you have consecrated your life and your ministry to the Lord, expect Him to give you the desires of your heart.

God is at work in you both to will and to do of His good pleasure! And His good pleasure is to reach the lost at any cost — to touch them, to teach them, to tell them what Jesus has done for them. That is *His* desire, not yours!

Do you have a heartfelt *desire* to be on the foreign field, to live in another culture, to see Christ formed in a people of another nation, to learn their language, and to love them with the Gospel? If you do, friend, *that* is a call! For the missionary, perhaps more than any other ministry, it may be said, "Home is where the heart is!" And if your heart is overseas, you'll never be satisfied anywhere else.

I am personally convinced that praying in the Spirit is one of the best ways to receive direction and confirmation from the Lord. As you take quality time to pray in the Holy Ghost, divine direction will begin to rise up in your spirit, giving illumination to your mind. Those things that God has placed within your heart to do will grow stronger.

You may receive specific guidance or only a more distinct impression or leading in your spirit. In either event, it is supernatural direction from the Spirit of God, and you can rely upon it. You can begin to take some *steps*. You will not get the full picture, but you will get enough to act upon.

Getting Ready To Go

1. **Spiritual Preparation.** The best spiritual preparation for the mission field is Bible school. At RHEMA, we were taught the Word of God and the operation of the Spirit of God. We were instructed in both the practical and the spiritual aspects of ministry. After graduation, we were given an opportunity to receive ministerial credentials and to become a part of an international ministerial organization.

   While at RHEMA, we developed relationships with students and staff that have proven to be a mainstay in our ministry today. Without a doubt, receiving formal instruction in the Word of God is the most important first step you can take in preparing to go to the field.

   Faithful service in any capacity in your local church is a must for the would-be missionary. *"For they that have used the office of a deacon well purchase to themselves a good degree [standing], and great boldness in the faith which is in Christ Jesus"* (1 Tim. 3:13).

   You prove yourself by serving in the local church. You also develop a track record for faithfulness that will follow you to the field in more ways than one.

   Finally, it goes without saying that time spent waiting on God is invaluable preparation.

   Mary and I took much time to wait upon God and to pray in the Spirit concerning our future ministry. Many people do not take the time to pray out the plan of God for their lives. And yet it can make the difference between keeping divine appointments and missing them! When you arrive on a new field where the people have never heard the Gospel, where there are no other believers, no churches, and you don't speak the language, you will need divine appointments!

   Take time to pray in the Holy Ghost about your future ministry!

2. **Natural Preparation.** From a natural standpoint, there are several things you can and should do to become ready to go to a foreign field, not the least of which is to develop a budget and to raise support. Those two subjects merit individual attention and are discussed later in the chapter. The following are some other matters to consider.

You will need to find someone reliable to handle both your ministry and personal matters in your absence. In the beginning, you may use a volunteer. In the long run, however, consider making it a paid position. First, it can involve a fair amount of work. Second, paid personnel tend to be more responsive to your needs than volunteers. A general power of attorney should be executed giving this person authority to handle your affairs.

Do your best to determine the types of clothing and supplies you will need on the field throughout the year as well as their availability. In the shops in our part of Russia, we have a very meager selection of inferior quality goods. Simple things like paper clips, Scotch tape, sponges, cleaning products, color film, batteries, light bulbs, and toilet paper — you name it — are seldom or never available in our shops.

If you buy clothes in America for your children, don't forget to plan for sudden growth spurts! The watchword is "plan ahead"! A short-term trip to your field can pay handsome dividends in this regard.

Before you leave the U.S., get physical and dental examinations for the whole family. You should also obtain a sound policy of health insurance coverage. You might also consider a will naming a guardian for your minor children, and possibly obtaining some life insurance.

Policies of term life insurance can be purchased relatively inexpensively. Some health insurance policies include a small life insurance benefit as part of the plan. There are companies which provide health insurance coverage specifically for missionaries. So budget for health insurance — it's not unbelief! Nothing can bring you off the field faster than financial failure.

If you increase the deductible, you lower the monthly premium. Pick a plan and deductible that suit your individual needs. Be sure that the plan will cover you both overseas and while Stateside.

Look closely at the policy to understand how it will work, what the deductible is for expenses incurred Stateside, to what extent medical evacuation expenses to the U.S. are covered, and whether the policy favors expenses being incurred Stateside or overseas. In many foreign countries, the cure is worse than the condition, and you will want to go home to the U.S. for medical treatment.

Finally, making strides toward the mastery of the language where you will be serving is always time well spent! Learning a language is time-consuming, and the ideal situation is to be able to devote yourself completely to language study *before* you assume ministerial duties on the field. Studying a foreign language in the U.S. rarely results in fluency, but it can give you a significant head start in that direction once you get to the field and begin to hear the language spoken on a consistent basis.

3. **Family Considerations.** If God has called you to the mission field, He has also called your family. It was a great comfort to me to realize that God's calling upon my life was inextricably bound up with His calling upon the lives of our children. None of us lives unto himself. By answering and fulfilling your call to the mission field, you are not depriving your children; you are helping them to fulfill their destiny in God!

The very best you can give your children in life, and the greatest heritage you can leave them, is to obey God. In the end, missionary kids are never deprived. God will see to it. He will repay them! Tell your children that.

Our children have a confidence based upon the Word of God and their own experience that God will multiply back to them what they are sowing into the Kingdom of God.

Obviously, a husband and wife must be in agreement to go to the mission field. Marital discord will undermine your effectiveness in any type of ministry, but perhaps more so on the foreign field. There are many subtle and not-so-subtle pressures that arise when you are living under the kinds of conditions encountered overseas. Work on having a good marriage. Pray together. Communicate.

It takes a special woman who is willing to forego the satisfaction of having her own home to have the opportunity to reach the unreached of the world.

When we made the decision to live and minister overseas, my wife had confidence that I was being led of the Spirit, and above all, her heart was to serve the Lord Jesus Christ. Consequently, she was willing to follow me and bring our four small children to the ends of the earth — which is exactly where we are! It would be impossible to be here with anything less than that kind of total dedication and consecration on her part.

If possible, take a trip to the field in advance of the family's arrival in order to locate clean and affordable housing and to ensure that you have adequate household goods and furniture to set up housekeeping.

Wives, if your husband makes that trip without you, give him a list of things to do! I found an apartment, but when I got home, I couldn't tell Mary whether there were any dishes, bedding, or beds! Also, get a national to negotiate for you in your absence, so that you are not charged "American" prices!

Regarding education, school-age children have the ability to learn languages rapidly, and mingling with other children at school not only accelerates their learning of the language, it also affords them the opportunity to make friends and be a Christian witness at school. However, it also affords them the opportunity to fall behind if the language is difficult or the local program is not ideal.

We opted for home schooling because we wanted our children to be solidly established in the rudiments of English grammar, literature, and American history, and to have the benefit of a Bible-based curriculum. If you choose to have your children attend a local school, you may want to supplement their education with home-school materials while they are overcoming the language barrier.

There are excellent Christian home-school materials available in the United States. Used home-school materials in excellent condition often can be purchased at a substantial discount through your state Christian home-school association or through a Christian school that is sensitive to the needs of missionaries.

The secret to success in home schooling is to obtain a curriculum that comes prepackaged together with teachers' manuals and lesson plans. The people who most often fail at home schooling are those who try to pull materials from here and there and put together their own program. That works for some people; for many it does not.

You will be amazed at how "routine" life can become for your family in another country. Your family will be a great witness for Christ there. One judge told me, "I received Jesus because when I saw that you had brought your dearest treasure — your family — into these conditions, I knew that you were sincere!"

4. **Business and Legal Considerations.** To be or not to be (incorporated)? That is the question! Unless you go as a "tent-maker" and work a secular job, there are essentially two ways to go to the mission field: 1) have *your own* tax-exempt, non-profit corporation; 2) receive offerings through *another* tax-exempt organization. Let's look at each option, considering the pros and cons:

A. **Incorporation.** Whether or not you incorporate your ministry depends in part on what God has called you to do. It also depends upon legal and tax considerations that are beyond the scope of this article. Suffice it to say, you should consult a legal or tax expert concerning your particular situation.

In seeking advice from a lawyer or an accountant, find one well versed in the law pertaining to religious, tax-exempt organizations. Most lawyers and accountants, even those who work regularly with business corporations, are unfamiliar with this unique and specialized area. You will find that an initial consultation often can be obtained for a minimum fee or sometimes for no fee at all.

You incorporate under the laws of your particular state. If you want to be able to guarantee that offerings to your ministry are tax-deductible to the donor (and you do!), you must also apply to the Internal Revenue Service for tax-exempt status under section 501(c)(3) of the Internal Revenue Code.

I know of many people who did this themselves, and you certainly could; however, although I had practiced law for 11 years, we hired a lawyer and an accountant to handle these matters for us. There are pitfalls for the unwary in the realm of non-profit corporate tax law!

Once you incorporate, you must maintain the corporation. You must form a board composed of members with wisdom and sound business judgment. Actions of the board must be memorialized in written minutes. In some states, certain board meetings can be conducted "by mail."

You must follow the laws of your state and the bylaws of the corporation, and you must be careful to distinguish between *your* property and the corporation's property, *your* funds and those belonging to the corporation. You may NOT comingle your funds with those of the corporation, nor utilize its property for your personal use.

There is a myriad of state and federal forms, filings, reports, and withholdings that must be made in a timely fashion for the corporation and its employees (that means you!). You should implement a calendaring system for these deadlines, and you would be wise to calendar them in *advance* of the due date.

Your lawyer or tax accountant will help you with all of these details. He or she can also suggest to you an easy system for maintaining your corporate financial records.

Obviously, you cannot do all of these things from the field. You must implement a system to see that these things are done in your absence, and you must have a responsible and knowledgeable person to do it for you. We prepared a ministry manual which details nearly every aspect of the business aspects of our ministry. It is a handy reference manual for our stateside administrator.

There are sound and good reasons to incorporate. Incorporation can help people to identify with your ministry. There can be certain tax advantages to incorporating. For example, the corporation can purchase health insurance for you so that you do not have to purchase health insurance with your personal taxable income. Another advantage is that you retain control and oversight over all the operations of the ministry.

We decided to incorporate for several reasons. We knew that incorporating would help people to identify with our mission. Our stateside office is in Alaska, and we are serving in the far northeastern corner of Siberia — not exactly a convenient location for doing banking, shopping, or the other practical aspects of ministry!

We knew we would need our own stateside administrator close at hand. Our own corporation was also a useful vehicle for accomplishing our long-range goal of raising up a team of missionaries. All things considered, incorporation seemed to be the best route for us.

B. Missionary agencies. The second way to go to the mission field is through another tax-exempt missionary organization. There are basically two kinds of missionary agencies: *service* agencies and *sending* agencies.

Generally, service agencies receive tax-deductible offerings in your behalf and send out your offering acknowledgment letters. Sometimes they will also send out your newsletter and will even prepare it for you based upon information you supply to them.

Most *service* agencies charge a fee; a few do not. Fees range in amount, but 10 percent of offerings received is customary. That amount is not unfair, particularly if the agency prepares the newsletter, mails it out, and pays the postage. Other service agencies, such as churches, will receive your offerings, send out the offering acknowledgment letters, and transmit your funds to you at no charge.

Service agencies do not assert control over the activities of the missionary, except that they are required to determine that funds disbursed to the missionary are used for purposes which promote and further the tax-exempt purpose of the service organization.

Sending agencies generally are formed with a specific ministry mission in mind. They, too, will receive offerings, send out offering letters, and send out newsletters on your behalf. In addition, they assist the missionary in going to the field and in getting established there.

Generally, they more or less retain control over the missionary, who is sent to the field to fulfill the vision of the sending organization. Often the missionary is expected to tithe his offering income or otherwise contribute to the general fund of the organization.

One can readily see the advantages of a service or sending agency over incorporation, particularly for the new or inexperienced missionary just getting started in the ministry. It is simpler. Some, but not all, of the administrative burden is shifted.

In large part, whether you incorporate or go through a service or sending agency, will depend upon what God has called you to do. Even if you sense that God has called you to have your own ministry, you might consider starting out with either a service or a sending agency until you gain experience and see the direction your ministry takes.

Drawbacks to working through some sending and service agencies include a lack of personal contact between the missionary and his partners and a perception of anonymity. If the agency has a ministry name, people tend to identify with the organization instead of with you and your ministry.

That problem can be overcome in part by taking the time to write a postcard or personal note to your partners periodically. When you start out in the ministry, this can be done easily by writing to a few people on your mailing list every day or every week. In this way, your partners will hear from you personally several times a year.

5. **Ministry Finances.** For the missionary candidate, particularly one with a family, the prospect of raising the support required to be on the field can look as formidable as Mount Everest! You will need to use your faith, and to your faith, add knowledge! The following are some simple, practical steps that you can take that will help you achieve your goals.

   A. **Develop a budget.** A budget is a goal-setting device; it also helps you maintain control over spending by setting limits. To prepare your budget, simply estimate as accurately and specifically as you can what your anticipated expenses will be for the coming year, taking into account both your stateside and overseas expenses.

   You will want to include categories for housing, food, clothing, utilities, telephone, home school, health insurance, life insurance, airfare, other transportation, postage, office supplies and expenses, personnel expenses, personal savings, and a miscellaneous category for unknown and unanticipated expenses for the year. Add up all your expenses, divide by twelve, and you will have a good idea of how much support you need monthly and annually!

   Be conservative in evaluating whether you have sufficient finances. Generally, people are so eager to get on the field that they leave as soon as they have "just enough" support. But in order to *stay* on the field, you will need to have *more than enough* support! People sometimes fail to keep their commitments to support you. Churches can close. You will have unanticipated expenses. Your vision and your ministry will expand. You need enough support to keep moving forward with your vision.

   As you maintain the forward momentum of your ministry, it becomes easier and easier to maintain the level of support you require. Consider raising at least 15 to 25 percent more support than you think you'll need, at least until you've had time to verify the accuracy of your budget.

   B. **Raising support.** Hudson Taylor, the great missionary to China, used to say, "God's work, done God's way, will never lack God's supply." To know that the responsibility for raising your support rests not with you but with God will set you free from one of the greatest hindrances to the missionary. That one truth can change your whole attitude toward itinerating and raising support.

   We began raising support by sending a newsletter to our family and friends and to people we had gotten to know at RHEMA who wanted to stay in touch with us. I contacted some pastors who had been students at RHEMA with me to see if they would be interested in having me come and share our vision. I always offered to come at my own expense on a free-will offering basis and never failed to cover my expenses and receive enough to bless our ministry besides.

   We made a point of attending our RMAI regional meetings and other meetings at RHEMA whenever we could. Although it was expensive to travel to those meetings all the way from Alaska, in the long run, they more than paid for themselves in terms of increased partners and monthly support, not to mention the spiritual refreshing we received.

Our RMAI regional meetings gave me a good chance to get to know the pastors in our region. They gladly had me come and share our vision with them. Some of them even helped to arrange other meetings for me! We had business cards and simple brochures printed so that when requested, they could be put in the hands of people interested in our ministry.

We also asked people on our mailing list to let others know about us. We printed up some "Partner Commitment and Newsletter Request" cards so that when we itinerate, it is easy for people in the churches to sign up to request the newsletter or to become a new partner with the ministry.

As doors begin to open, you will have the opportunity to share your vision in other local churches. Many missionaries dread itinerating. To be honest with you, I do not! It is a refreshing opportunity to minister in English, without an interpreter, and I enjoy my fellowship with the pastors. I listen to them and learn from them, as most of them have been in the ministry longer than I have.

These pastors have been extremely sensitive to the challenges of missionary life, and as a group they have not only supported us financially, they have embraced the needs of our entire family as well. What a difference that makes to the missionary on the field!

We never put pressure on people or churches to give. We do not ask for money. We simply share what the Lord is doing through us and give folks an opportunity to become a part of it. Some do and some don't, but I go with the confidence that there are people who are called to support us, and I simply trust the Lord to speak to their hearts.

If you can demonstrate to your partners that you are making visible progress toward your goal *while* you are raising support, it will be a great benefit in every way. Your partners will be encouraged, you will be encouraged, and the vision will move forward.

One way to do this is to take a short-term trip to the field. It will provide you with a wealth of information. It also will help spark the vision in your own heart and keep it alive during this most trying stage of your ministry. In turn, you can inspire your partners afresh and anew with what God has called you to do.

Short-term mission trips give you a track record and credibility. They help open doors for you to share your vision. And your partners will be encouraged to see that you are making progress toward your goal!

It is important to realize that your ministry will develop gradually, little by little. It is critical that you realize the importance of taking steps of faith as you are led by the Spirit. It causes the finances you need to come in and demonstrates visible, forward progress in your ministry to your partners.

Your Newsletter

Partnership is based upon relationship, and those relationships begin to form as you share your vision and people get to know you. In establishing and maintaining a relationship with your partners, it is absolutely essential that you *communicate* with them diligently and frequently.

One of the main reasons people stop supporting missionaries is that they seldom, if ever, hear from them!

A newsletter is one of the most effective ways of sharing your vision, of staying in communication with your partners, and of maintaining accountability to them. Start by sending it to people who know you and who would be interested in hearing about what you are doing.

Unsolicited newsletters to pastors and others who do not know you are generally ill-advised and ineffective. However, don't hesitate to encourage in a gracious manner those who know you to pass along your newsletters and to tell others about your ministry. Little by little, your contacts — and your base of support — will begin to grow.

Be consistent with the timing of your newsletter, whether you send it out quarterly, bimonthly, or monthly. During the month, jot down ideas for the next issue. When it comes to writing the newsletter, there are all kinds of different styles, formats, and methods. Take a look at other missionaries' newsletters to get some ideas for yourself.

Certainly you want to present your newsletter attractively with a minimum of expenditure. And with a modicum of effort, you can utilize a wide variety of desktop publishing techniques. However, I want to suggest to you that the most important aspect of your newsletter will not be the graphics you employ or the format you choose, but that you be yourself.

Another minister once asked me, "What would you advise someone about how to write a newsletter?" I found myself answering, "I just write from my heart!" Do that, and you'll do well! Simply "talk" to your partners through your newsletter.

Although you must share the vision with your partners in general, when it comes to specifics, you are better off to report what you *have done* as opposed to what you are *thinking* of doing. There are so many variables on the mission field that things have a way of not working out as you had planned!

To a degree that they may never realize, your partners are an integral part of your ministry. You are an extension of their ministry! That kind of relationship requires and is nurtured by communication.

To fulfill the call of God upon your life, you must write the vision and make it plain, not just for yourself but also for your partners, for God will not call you to the mission field alone. He will raise up people to support you, to pray for you, and to encourage you.

Your partners need to be encouraged in the vision as well, so you must involve them. They must hear what you hear, see what you see, and feel what you feel. You are accountable to them and to the Lord. It is absolutely essential that you maintain a vital communication link with your partners.

Developing a Ministry on the Foreign Field

There are three ways to develop a ministry on foreign soil. The *first* is to go assist an existing work by a national minister; the *second* is to go assist an existing work by a foreign missionary who is already established on the field; and the *third* is to go to establish your own work.

The first two have several obvious advantages over the third, not the least of which is the opportunity to work under and to learn from a seasoned missionary or a national minister. Had that option been available to us, I would preferred to have gone that route, but we are the only Full-Gospel ministry in our particular area of Russia.

In establishing your own work, frequently you start out with only a very general sense of the direction God is leading you, and as you begin to take some steps of faith, more specific direction comes. That was the case with the Apostle Paul as the Spirit led him to go into Macedonia in Acts 16:6-15.

As with Paul, sometimes you find out where you're *not* supposed to go! Even so, that is direction! I especially like Proverbs 4:12 in the Hebrew version. It reads, "As thou goest, thy way shall be opened up step by step before thee."

We certainly have found that to be true! After graduating from RHEMA, I wanted to go directly to the mission field, but there were two obstacles. First, I did not know where to go, and, second, people were not lining up at our door to become partners with our ministry!

The only leading I had was to accept an offer for a part-time position as associate pastor of our home church in Wasilla, Alaska. It seemed to me at the time that it was the opposite direction of the one in which I wanted to go, but it witnessed with us, so we obeyed. We sold our car to pay our airfare back to Alaska, and landed there with just about enough money to feed our family for one month, and that was it!

It was after that one step of obedience that God's financial provision began to pour in. We still had no partners, but we were abundantly provided for, and without knowing it, we were being positioned to be able to leave for the foreign field.

A few months after returning to Alaska, I began to travel out to the remote Indian and Eskimo villages in the arctic and subarctic regions of the state to minister. With every trip to the bush, I gained experience and confidence about following the witness of the Spirit when stepping out into new territories without contacts. It was also during this period that we began sending out a newsletter, and our base of support began to develop.

Finally, in June 1990, the Lord put it into my heart that I could go into Russia from Alaska. At the time, I did not even know if it was possible! A short time later, with the help of an Eskimo reindeer-herder's wife in Nome, Alaska, I obtained a letter of invitation from a family in Provideniya.

I made my first trip there alone. I knew no one and almost no Russian. There were few real believers, if any. However, I went with an inward confidence in my heart because I had a witness in my spirit to go. Everything I had learned by traveling out to the villages in bush Alaska during the preceding one and a half years came into play on that trip. Very often, receiving direction is simply a matter of following the Spirit of God by taking each step as He shows it to you!

We did not set out to pioneer a work in Chukotka. In all, I made three trips to Provideniya and a fourth trip to another part of Russia before my wife and I and our four children moved to Provideniya in September 1992 to pioneer a church.

During each trip I took to Russia, more and more people prayed to receive Christ. We began to have a growing concern about those who had heard the Gospel as a result of our ministry, but who had no pastor to care for them or teach them.

We really had no spectacular guidance at any time to move to Russia. From the time we moved back to Alaska after graduating from RHEMA and began traveling out to the bush, we simply continued to follow the inward witness of the Holy Spirit in our hearts.

Gradually, we moved out in an ever-widening circle of ministry until we reached Provideniya. Although we had no spectacular guidance, we did have the supernatural witness of the Holy Spirit in our spirits and confirmation all along the way that the Lord was leading us. Of course, I might add that we had our share of obstacles and difficulties along the way!

In determining a location for our mission within Chukotka, several factors combined caused us to settle on Provideniya. First, a great and effectual door of utterance was opened to us in Chukotka. Second, as we ministered to the people of northeastern Siberia, they became more and more on our hearts.

It was in our hearts to go to them, and it was not in our hearts to go anywhere else! Third, Provideniya was a chief city in our particular region, easily accessible from Alaska. Fourth, we had a settled peace in our hearts that Provideniya was to be our "home" for a while.

Since there was virtually no evangelical presence in most of the cities and villages in our region, it was easy to pick a target audience for our ministry there: *simply everyone*! Our primary goal at first was to plant a church there so that the believers could be fed on the Word of God and be taught the full Gospel.

Since then, we have used many avenues to preach the Gospel, including radio and television, plus ministry in the kindergarten, elementary, and high schools, the boarding school/orphanage, in the technical school, in the hospital, and on the military base. We also conducted outreaches to various villages.

One particularly effective outreach has been the distribution of approximately 4,500 of Rev. Kenneth E. Hagin's books translated into the Russian language. We have also distributed medical supplies, vitamins, and a modest amount of financial aid.

For a few years before coming to Russia, we sensed that the Lord might have us develop a team of missionaries. We tried to do something with that while still in Alaska, but it really did not begin to take shape until after our second year in Provideniya. It was then that we began to support other missionaries, particularly Russians, on a consistent basis in order to help reach the villages and cities in Chukotka.

This concept is still developing, but we and our church in Provideniya now support in whole or in part a team of four American missionaries (including my wife and me) and two Russian missionaries as well as a seventh missionary in another city from time to time.

Our goal is to support a missionary until he becomes self-supporting, so that we can then divert the funds previously used to support him to bring the next missionary onto the field.

Of course, we know that this is the general direction in which the Lord is leading us, and that as we could continue to walk in the light of what we know, more insight and further direction will continue to come!

Feed Your Faith To Conquer Challenges and Obstacles

It was said of Hudson Taylor that he considered the greatest challenge facing the missionary was that of maintaining time for consistent, prayerful meditation in the Word. There will be many things that come up along the way to challenge and even to prevent you from bringing the Gospel to the people to whom God sends you. It may be persecution, poor living conditions, a language barrier, bad water, or just discouragement!

However, if you will take the time to feed your own faith by meditating in the Word, praying in the Spirit, reading faith-inspiring books, and listening to good teaching tapes, none of those things will move you. Kenneth Hagin Ministries' monthly missions packet and "Ministers' Manna" are two great ways to make sure that you are feeding your own spirit regularly.

Some Final Thoughts

I will never forget something that happened on the first evening of my first trip to Provideniya. The people there said to me that after 70 years of atheistic communism, they wanted to believe in God, but it was very difficult for them because they had been trained as materialists from their youth on.

So for the next several days, I taught them from the Word of God, showing them from the Scriptures who Jesus is, why He came, and that apart from Christ, men are without hope and without God in this world. Finally, on the last evening, it began to dawn on them that they were in a lost condition, and that they must be born again.

At that point, a woman looked up at me with tears in her eyes and said, "How wonderful that you came! It is as though we were blind, and now our eyes have been opened. There you were in a different country and with your own life, and God sent you to us!"

To me that is the essence of the missionary call. We are ambassadors of Christ, by whom God is beseeching the world to be reconciled to Him! If you are called to missions, don't be deterred by the obstacles! Determine within yourself that you *will* make it to the mission field. Don't allow yourself to be talked out of your call. If you are called to be a missionary, you will not be happy doing anything else, and any sacrifice you make in order to take the Gospel to the world will be far exceeded by the rewards you gain for having gone!

Chapter 5
Moving to the Mission Field —
Our Greatest Adventure!

By Larry ('87 '88) and Angela Keeton ('92)

Larry and Angela Keeton are the founders and pastors of *Krestanske Centrum Viry* (Faith Christian Center) in Prague, Czech Republic, and are also the directors of *Domata Centrum Biblickeho Studia* (Domata Center for Biblical Studies), a school to train national ministers. They moved to the Czech Republic in 1992.

Prior to this time, they worked at RHEMA Bible Church/Kenneth Hagin Ministries, aka RHEMA Bible Training Center, for several years. Larry is a 1988 graduate of the training center. Angela earned a seminary degree in 1977 and in 1992 received an honorary diploma from RBTC, where she taught several classes.

Together, Larry and Angela taught a singles School of the Bible class (Sunday school) at RHEMA Bible Church. Larry also traveled as an evangelist after working at RBC for four years. Angela worked at RBC for 10 years as administrative assistant to Rev. and Mrs. Kenneth Hagin Jr., and as an instructor at the training center.

Our journey to the mission field began long before we actually arrived there. It was a step for which we had both been in preparation for many years.

As early as 1975 during her own Bible school days, Angela had missions on her heart along with teaching in a Bible school, but the time was never right to go. Then during 1983 and 1984 while working at RHEMA, she regularly attended weekly prayer meetings for Russia and eastern Europe conducted on the RHEMA campus by Rev. Kenneth E. Hagin. Her heart became drawn toward eastern Europe.

When Larry was born again in 1983, he told the Lord, "I'll go anywhere and do anything for You, but if You give me a choice, I'd rather not go to the mission field!"

However, this attitude completely changed in 1988 when as a student at RHEMA, Larry went on a home-missions trip to the Navajo Indian reservation. While he was there, God dealt with his heart about missions. Shortly after he returned from that trip, the two of us met and were married later that year. We both knew from the beginning that we would eventually serve God together overseas.

In 1990, we took a missions trip together to Austria, Hungary, and Romania. We were never the same again! Our hearts were moved with compassion at the conditions we witnessed in eastern Europe and at the tremendous need for the Gospel in the eastern European nations.

Over the next year and a half, Larry made two more trips into eastern Europe to what was then Czechoslovakia, staying a month on each trip. Throughout this time, the vision for a Bible school in eastern Europe started to form in our hearts. After his second trip, we began to seriously pray about moving to eastern Europe.

A mutual friend suggested we talk with Mark and Janet Brazee, who also had European Bible schools in their hearts. After meeting with Mark and Janet and spending much time in prayer, the plan of God became clear. We knew we were to move to Prague, Czechoslovakia, to start and direct a Bible school, working in conjunction with the Brazees. Larry also had it in his heart to pioneer a church in Prague.

We did not know anyone in Prague and didn't have any other missionaries there to help us when we arrived. In short, we were setting out on the biggest adventure of our lives!

Preparation Is *Essential* — Especially in Moving Overseas

With only six months to prepare for our move, we found ourselves caught up in a blur of activity. At that time, Larry was a traveling minister and had meetings already scheduled until two months before we were to leave. Angela's final day of work at Kenneth Hagin Ministries would be just a little over a month before our scheduled departure. Apart most of the time and working full-time jobs, we were faced with a major task such as neither of us had undertaken before, and we could find very little information to help us know how to proceed.

Through much prayer, we had already been preparing spiritually for this move, but now our prayers became more focused. We endeavored to "pray out" the will of God as much as possible before we actually arrived on the field. We began to pray, speak the Word, and believe for specific things we knew we would need, such as finances, a place to live, interpreters, transportation, students, favor, etc.

We firmly believed then, and have become even more convinced since arriving on the mission field, that faith in God's Word is our most valuable asset. Faith is more important than the American Express card — don't leave home without it!

Even though spiritual preparations were underway, we were still faced with a hundred natural questions and decisions. It seemed that every day there was something new to deal with.

For example, we knew we needed to ship our goods to Prague, but how? What was involved in clearing Czech customs once we arrived? What should we take and what should we leave behind? What about health insurance? What kinds of things did we need to plan for in our budget? How should we go about raising finances? What about our families we would be leaving behind?

Having faced these concerns ourselves, we trust that our experiences and observations can benefit others who will be making the transition to the mission field.

Practical Aspects Must Not Be Overlooked

After contacting about 15 different shipping companies, we learned that we had many options and price ranges. We could pack our goods ourselves and drive them overland to a coastal city where they could be shipped from the U.S. either to Prague or, more commonly, to a neighboring country. From there, we would have to pick them up and get them to Prague ourselves.

Or we could arrange door-to-door delivery from our home in Oklahoma to Prague, with the moving company doing a lot of the packing and unpacking. We chose this option even though it was more expensive. Without any contacts in the Czech Republic, we didn't know how to transport our goods from another city or country into Prague.

The cheapest option (had it been available to us) would have been container shipping, especially if we could have shared a container with a company or another family going to the same destination. We would advise prospective missionaries to contact several different shippers, ask a lot of questions, and get all the possible options before making a decision. There can be a sizable difference in prices!

What about clearing customs in your destination country? We found that U.S. shippers could tell us virtually nothing about Czech customs regulations or possible costs we would face. The Czechoslovakian embassy in Washington D.C. and the American embassy in Prague were only slightly more helpful, but we were to later find that some of the information they gave us was incorrect.

Your best source may be another American missionary or American family within your destination country. We say "American" because customs regulations for nationals from other countries may be different from those for Americans.

We learned that our best route would have been to ship our goods in care of an established church or organization within the country to avoid customs charges. Unfortunately, we didn't have anyone to ship our goods to! Shipping 2,000 pounds of goods, we were hit with a $3,000 customs charge upon the arrival of our shipment in Prague!

Thank God for faith! We prayed and found favor with the Dutch moving company who handled the European portion of our move. They talked Czech customs down to $500 and arranged to have our money refunded once we registered our organization with the Czech government!

Obtaining health insurance was another obstacle we faced. We did not think it fair to be a potential burden on our families, our supporters, or the nationals we were going to minister to by failing to provide for ourselves some type of health coverage. Again, our advice would be to check several companies. We found that companies would insure us for short-term trips, but very few would insure us to actually live in another country.

From the outset, however, we were very honest about our intentions to relocate overseas. We didn't want coverage to be later denied because the company mistakenly thought we were living Stateside.

Another option for health coverage might be to obtain medical insurance or coverage within the destination country. This would, of course, depend on several factors, such as the quality of medical care within the country, the cost, the requirements for foreigners to be eligible, etc. Again, your best source of information may well be other Americans living within the country.

What kinds of things should you ship overseas? Our advice would be this: Don't pay to ship anything you can obtain at a reasonable price and quality within the destination country itself. If you can contact someone within the country, you can learn what kinds of furniture, appliances, household goods, vehicles, staple food items, toiletries, and so forth, are available, along with their general costs.

Save your valuable shipping space for things that can't be obtained in the country, such as study books and tapes, items needed for your ministry, and items of a personal nature.

One thing we took for which we have been continually grateful was a stackable washer and dryer wired for 220 volts. These and other 220-volt appliances are obtainable Stateside. Washers and dryers in other countries can be very small compared with their U.S. counterparts.

We also took large step-down transformers from which we could run 110-volt electrical items that we took with us. We also took converter plugs to adapt appliances to different types of receptacle outlets.

Make Your Overseas Home a Haven

Another important consideration is the appearance of your home. Veteran missionaries once gave us advice that has proven to be invaluable. They said, "Make your home on the field as much like America (or your own home country) as you can within reason. Don't try to live like the nationals do. They don't expect it, and you may even lose their respect by trying to do so.

"Every day you will be continually immersed in a different language, culture, and way of thinking. Your home needs to be a sanctuary where you and your family are in familiar, comfortable surroundings."

We took their advice. We put stateside touches in our apartment like family pictures, American-style bedding, and decorations and wall hangings from the U.S., interspersed with some of the things we like from the Czech culture. It is a place in which we truly feel peaceful and comfortable. We can study, pray, and get away from it all in the refuge of our home.

Budgeting, Fund-Raising, Faith, and Other Essentials!

When it came time to plan our budget, we included the following items as one-time start-up expenses: the cost of shipping our goods, airline tickets, deposit on an apartment, furniture, appliances, household goods, basic equipment for our church, and a new or used vehicle.

Our monthly budget began first of all with tithes and offerings. Some missionaries feel they don't need to give since all of their income is designated for ministry anyway. But that is not true! Your sources will dry up if you don't give! We tithe into our local church here in Prague. Also, we support another missionary monthly and give to several others as needs arise. We help with expenses for some of our students and are also Kenneth Hagin Ministries' Word Partner Club members.

We've determined to be channels of financial blessing for the Gospel's sake. We believe the saying is true, "If God can get it *through* you, He will get it *to* you."

Other monthly budget items included rent, utilities, food, postage, health insurance, transportation expenses within the country (automobile fuel or bus or train costs), phone, any stateside expenses in our absence, personal items, clothing, ministry expenses, and allocation of funds for a round-trip ticket to the U.S.

You may not know until you're actually on the field how much you'll need for ministry expenses, so you may have to prayerfully set an *estimated* figure of what you think you will spend for things like literature, building rental or purchase, equipment, salaries for national helpers, etc.

In raising financial support, ours was a unique situation in that we had only six months between the time we knew with finality we were moving until our scheduled departure date. From the beginning of our marriage, we had known we would eventually be going overseas, so we had worked to become debt-free. Therefore, we owed nothing but a house payment.

Although Larry already had meetings scheduled in several churches, he had scheduled these before he knew we would be going to the mission field. Since they were scheduled for the purpose of ministry to the various congregations, we did not feel it was right to turn them into missions fund-raisers.

So we just did what we knew to do in the natural and trusted God to do the rest. We saw nothing wrong with telling people what we planned to do. That way, they could get involved financially if they desired to do so. We informed people around us through word-of-mouth and sent letters to everyone we knew who lived elsewhere.

In sharing our plans with others, we kept it as low-key as possible. We didn't want to put pressure on anyone to give. We had decided when we got married that we would always make God our source, not man. Since then, we've been so glad we made that choice early!

We got exactly three responses to our letter: Angela's parents, Larry's best friend, and a man who had already been sending support for Larry's traveling ministry! Needless to say, those finances did not even begin to supply what we needed. Time passed and there was little change in our situation. From the money we had, we went ahead and purchased our airline tickets.

With one month left before we were to leave, no more income from our jobs, and our savings entirely depleted, we had about $200 a month in pledged support — not even enough to leave the country with! But we had been believing and speaking the Word and calling the money in. So we just continued to take steps in the direction we believed God was leading us and continued with our plans to leave.

We didn't hint to anyone else that the money we needed hadn't yet come in. Instead, we trusted God. Then about two to three weeks before our scheduled departure date, suddenly money began to come in from seemingly everywhere, and we had enough to go!

Someone might ask, "What would you have done if the money had not come in by the time you were to leave?" That's a good question. We would have continued to seek God, and if we *knew that we knew* He was telling us to go right then, we would have gone anyway. But if there had been an uneasiness in our hearts, we would have remained Stateside and continued to raise funds until we had enough to leave.

Often there is a fine line between faith and presumption — the difference comes in being truly led by the Spirit of God.

We've seen missionaries struggle financially on the field and have seen others have to return to the States due to lack of finances. That's extremely difficult both for the missionaries and for the nationals with whom they are working.

When you're trying to get started on the mission field, you don't need constant financial pressure. There's enough to deal with — adjusting to the culture, language, and lifestyle, as well as different ministry conditions and situations — without having to be under a financial burden.

We would strongly advise prospective missionaries to raise adequate support *prior* to leaving the U.S. unless they have a mandate from God to do otherwise.

In our experience, the majority of our financial support has come from totally unexpected sources. We've talked with other missionaries who have said the same thing. No matter who you are or who you know, God is still going to require you to live by faith.

Every month, we pray and agree for a specific amount of support, and then we thank God that it's coming in. When we receive that amount consistently for three to four months, we increase it. God is faithful! We say continually, "We'll never lack for finances, buildings, transportation, or any other resources we'll need to fulfill the will of God."

Maintaining Lines of Support Through Communication

Once support is raised, however, it must be maintained. One thing we believe has helped us in this area is that we are in constant contact with our contributors to let them know what we are doing on the field.

We've talked with pastors who've said that they rarely hear from some of their missionaries and have no idea what they are doing. That is not good. We need to be accountable to those who faithfully give of their prayers and finances to help us in our work.

Once and sometimes twice a month, our partners hear from us, either in the form of a report or a thank-you for their help. We know how busy the mission field can be. Something that might take a few minutes to transact in the States can be an all-day affair on the mission field. But we purposely make the time to keep in touch with our supporters. They are our co-laborers in the harvest, and we want them involved in what we are doing. They can be involved to a greater degree when they are informed.

Our business affairs are conducted primarily from Prague. The Brazees' office in Tulsa handles the receiving and receipting of finances from our contributors and sends us a monthly printout. We send acknowledgments, newsletters, and other correspondence from Prague. We handle all our stateside business affairs from here as well. Before we left Oklahoma, we set up as many stateside payments as we could on automatic bank drafts to make it easier for us.

We've had no reason or need to incorporate our ministry Stateside thus far, so we haven't. But we are registered in the Czech Republic, so we have a ministry board here composed of Czechs, Mark Brazee, and ourselves. We keep our church and school financial records on a computer bookkeeping program and keep minutes of our regular meetings. In case we should ever be questioned by the Czech authorities, all is in order.

Saying Good-Bye to Loved Ones

One area that was especially difficult for us in going to the mission field was the matter of leaving our family behind. We are very close to our family, and it pulled at our heartstrings tremendously to move so far from them. We know what it is to cry in airports after leaving our family (and sometimes for several days afterwards), but we also want to encourage anyone reading this book who may be struggling in this area: You will be a bigger help and blessing to your family *in* the will of God than *out of* the will of God!

You may be leaving behind elderly parents, unsaved family members, and so forth, but put them in God's hands. When we realized we were definitely moving to the Czech Republic, we made this determination: We are going to take care of God's business, and He is going to take care of our family. And He has! We, and other missionaries we know, have seen Him intervene to heal, prosper, and bring family members to salvation while we were on the other side of the world! He is faithful to His Word and to His people.

Establishing Your Ministry Through Faith and Patience

We knew that once we arrived in Prague, we were to establish a ministers' training center and a church. Now that we've been here awhile, other areas have been added to our vision as well, such as translating and printing books, cassette tape distribution, crusades, and church planting.

Vision is wonderful and very important, but it is implemented one day at a time, one step at a time. We have to exercise a lot of patience in implementing parts of our vision until God's timing is right and we have the personnel to help us.

The first step was to get the ministry established on a solid foundation. We wanted something that would last and not be a fly-by-night operation. We didn't want to get a ministry started and have it stopped by the authorities or have major roadblocks to overcome due to legalities. That meant registering our ministry with the Czech government.

Under the post-communist system, the registration process required mounds of paperwork, months of time, and incredible patience. At first, no one here seemed to know what we needed to do to register our ministry with the government. We spent days going all over Prague from one government office to another, only to reach a dead end and have to start all over. But finally, God led us to a Czech man who knew the procedure, and our ministry was registered — 10 months after we started!

We also obtained long-term residence visas. This, too, took faith because the requirements for a visa when we first arrived in the country filled an entire page. The requirements were virtually impossible. We prayed and said, "Lord, even if You have to change the laws, we believe we receive our visas."

Three months later, Czechoslovakia divided into two countries — the Czech Republic and Slovakia — and the requirements for visas totally changed! More paperwork and waiting ensued, but in six months' time, we had visas!

Another big challenge for us was being all alone without an interpreter for the first seven months we were in the country. God moved upon a woman in the U.S. at a church where Larry had ministered to take her vacation and be in Prague when we arrived. She was raised in Prague and still had friends here. Within two days of our arrival, she had found us an apartment — in a city where people had been on waiting lists for apartments for years! What a testimony to God's provision! But once she returned to the States, we were left without anyone to help us communicate.

That forced us to learn our way around the city and to use the language the best we could. We also got very good at charades! Finally, we found an interpreter and found a building to rent. We were ready to start our church, Faith Christian Center! We passed out 5,000 flyers door-to-door, distributed handbills in the subway, and showed the "Jesus" movie in Czech three times over a period of two weeks, leading up to our first Sunday. With all this groundwork, *no one* showed up for our first service. What did we do? We preached anyway, like the building was full! For our second service, we had two people.

Be Faithful To Do Your Part, and God Will Do His Part

Sometimes we hear overnight success stories from missionaries, and thank God for every one of them! But more times than not, missions work is just plain "toughing it out" through faith and patience. A year later, our church has just set a new attendance record with 48 people present, and leaders are starting to be produced out of our core group.

Domata Center for Biblical Studies followed the same pattern of development as did the church. This nine-month training school for ministers meets every day, Monday through Friday, for three and a half hours. We started the school one week after we started the church. Although we did all we knew to do to get students, the first year we had only six. And three of those applied on the last day that we could have accepted their applications — just in the nick of time!

But in this second year, our enrollment has almost tripled. And now last year's graduates are starting to produce fruit in the ministry. One graduate's church is exploding with new converts, and he is looking to start more churches in nearby villages. Already we're getting applications for next school year.

We've had to believe God for every student and every church member. All the time we were believing, it looked in the natural like we wouldn't have even one person to minister to. But God is true, and His Word never fails! Within the last six months, we've also been able to start printing Rev. Kenneth E. Hagin's books in the Czech language. Our progress hasn't been earthshaking. Instead, it has been slow and steady, but we can see that it is increasing in momentum over time.

All countries, and even cities within the same country, are different. There are different degrees of opposition from established churches or religions, different situations, different seasons of harvest. Some missionaries arrive in a country where others have plowed and prepared the way, and it's harvest time.

Others have to go in first and do the plowing and planting in order for there to be a harvest. Don't allow yourself to become discouraged or compare yourself with others in other places. You only need to answer this question: "Am I doing what God told me to do?"

If the answer is yes, continue to be faithful. Let God grow the work — that's His part. If you try to do God's part, you will frustrate yourself endlessly and be continually depressed. You can't grow the work, and even if you did, it would be worthless. Stay consistent, even if it looks like your labor is in vain and circumstances try to scream at you that it will never happen. God is for you, and He will reward your labors with increase.

The most challenging things we've had to deal with in our work have been attacks of discouragement, the language and cultural differences, feelings of isolation, and the fact that visible progress has not come as quickly as we desired.

This is where we've had to learn to encourage ourselves in the Lord. Praise, worship, and thanksgiving are tremendous tools in this area. It's hard to be discouraged while praising and thanking God. Anyone can shout *after* the walls have fallen, but when we really need to shout is when the walls loom before us like mountains.

Keeping our eyes on the Word has helped us stay consistent in doing the necessary work, seeing the end result rather than focusing on present circumstances. We have specific scriptures posted in our home that we regularly agree upon together for our personal lives and ministry. We keep Word-filled, joyful music playing in our house along with teaching tapes that minister to us personally in areas of faith, healing, victory, and so forth — and we stay busy!

The Importance of Fellowship On and Off the Field

We have sought out other missionaries to have fellowship with and have had friends from two different stateside groups. We haven't necessarily believed the same way they did on all Bible subjects, but we've recognized the importance of friendships.

We agreed with one couple not to talk about areas of doctrinal conflict but to focus instead on the points we could agree upon and to just enjoy each other's company. Being Americans and fellow Southerners as well gave us a lot in common. We had some great Mexican meals, exchanged useful business and ministry information, shared news from the States, and prayed for one another. We even helped them get a church started before we started our own.

If you're the first "word-of-faith" missionaries in a country or an area of a country and are apart from other English speakers like we were, feelings of isolation can be very real. Don't isolate yourself further by refusing to fellowship with missionaries from other groups. The Body of Christ is big and diverse, and every part is important — we need each other.

At least once, and sometimes twice a year, we fly back to the States. We include this expense in our budget, but by flying the same airline consistently, we are also able to earn free tickets with our frequent-flyer miles. We feel it is important to our own well-being to return Stateside periodically. If we don't stay built up, the ministry suffers the consequences. So we return for three primary purposes: to visit family, to be refreshed spiritually, and to visit churches that support us or indicate that they would like to have us visit.

In our schedule, we plan to attend meetings where we know we can be ministered to, and we spend time with other ministers in order to fellowship and to be "sharpened" by them. Also, we like to personally meet as many of the people who support us as we possibly can. In order to accomplish those things, we've learned the hard way that we must pace ourselves carefully during each trip. Otherwise, we return to the field exhausted only to jump back into a busy schedule, and that defeats the purpose for ever going to the States.

'If We Had It To Do All Over Again . . .'

The old saying goes, "Hindsight is better than foresight," and if we had it to do over, we'd definitely do some things differently. But primarily, we'd concentrate more on two areas: being more specific in prayer for certain helps personnel we would need and learning the language early.

If you know you will be going to a particular language group, start now to learn their language. Take courses or get tapes and begin learning as much as you can even before you leave the States. The more difficult the language, the longer it will take you to become conversant and eventually preach in that language. But it is important to learn the language. You cannot rely on an interpreter forever!

Also, "pray out" as much of the plan of God as you can before leaving the States, praying in other tongues and also in your understanding. Pray and believe for specific helps personnel you will need such as interpreters, musicians, secretaries, or children's workers. You will need them sooner than you think, and it's better to have them already waiting for you rather than your having to wait for them.

In addition, allow the Holy Spirit to help you pray for people and things you may not even know you need. Don't be concerned that by praying so much ahead of time, you'll leave yourself with no faith projects — there will be plenty of things left to pray for once you arrive in your destination country!

Other Considerations

In closing, if we could share something with those considering becoming a missionary, it would be this: The mission field, like any other area of ministry, requires hard work and stubborn persistence in the face of obstacles. Contrary to some people's thinking, the mission field is not glamorous. It is not a place to make an international name for oneself or a way to escape from a problematic or dissatisfying life in the States. Whatever problems a person has Stateside will probably be magnified on the mission field.

The mission field is definitely not a good place for those who have a troubled marriage or home life, as the pressures of a new culture and way of life will put additional strain on relationships.

A person must be certain God has called him to the mission field before packing and moving to another country. Relocating overseas is not something that is easily undone once it has been done, and there will be many opportunities to question why on earth you ever came! But every time the questions have come, we've been able to face the devil head-on because we know that we know that God has sent us. Therefore, we're not leaving until God says to go! Hearing from God makes all the difference.

We would also recommend being as debt-free as possible. In addition, it would be good to take an extended trip to the country where you want to serve before you actually move there. Anything can look good for a few days or a week, so be sure to give yourself time to get past the tourist or excitement stage. You need to really see the country, its living conditions, and the work that needs to be done there. It is foolish to move to the mission field simply on the basis of emotion or inspiration.

Educating yourself about the country and the need there and visiting it in person will give the Holy Spirit something to work with as you pray. Then pray until you are certain in your heart what God wants you to do and where and when He wants you to do it.

When going to the mission field, go with a servant's heart, willing to do anything to be a blessing there. Missions work is much more than just preaching and teaching. There is also a great deal of menial, physical labor that must be done. This is true whether you are starting your own ministry or are going to work with someone else. Determine ahead of time that no job will be beneath your "dignity" to perform and that you will work in any capacity needed. By having this attitude, you will be a great blessing on the mission field, and doors of ministry will readily open to you.

If relocating to the mission field is not God's plan for you, there are still many ways to be involved in missions — through short-term trips, praying, giving, and helping to educate others to the need for missions outreach.

On the other hand, if God is sending you to the mission field, an adventure awaits you! The fields of the world are white unto harvest, and the need for laborers has never been greater! Entire nations wait to be reached with the life-giving Gospel. God is already preparing the hearts of those you will minister to, and they will be ready for you when you arrive.

So go with confidence and boldness and a determination to stay until God's purpose is accomplished through you. We can promise you it will not always be easy, but you will experience great joy in giving the Word to those who have never heard it before.

We are in the beginning stages of the greatest revival in the history of the world. The glory of God is going to cover the earth, and He will manifest His glory through human vessels! So get in your place and be faithful. God will use you to change the course of peoples and nations!

Chapter 6
Recognizing, Developing, and Utilizing Your Call to Missions

By John Romick ('83 '84)

In 1980, John Romick earned a Bachelor of Science degree in Computer Science from National College of Rapid City, South Dakota. He graduated from RHEMA Bible Training Center in 1984 and within three months of graduation, left for the mission field in Quetzaltenango, Guatemala, where he met and married his wife, Alba.

In the fall of 1988, the Lord led the Romicks to Bogotá, Colombia. They are currently the directors of Mission Colombia, which consists of a local church, Bible schools, and a ministerial association.

John and Alba have two children: John David, age 5, and Daniel, age 2.

Missions — Teaching Faithful Men

2 TIMOTHY 2:2

2 And the things that thou hast heard of me among many witnesses, the same commit thou to faithful men, who shall be able to teach others also.

It has been said that the mission of missions is the Church, and the mission of the Church is missions. To me, at the very heart of missions is teaching faithful men who will in turn teach others. That's why we concentrate our missions work in the area of Bible schools, training centers, local churches, and so forth. We are now at the place in our ministry where most of the classes in our Bible school are taught by nationals.

ACTS 19:8-10

8 And he [Paul] went into the synagogue, and spake boldly for the space of three months, disputing and persuading the things concerning the kingdom of God.

9 But when divers were hardened, and believed not, but spake evil of that way before the multitude, he departed from them, and separated the disciples, disputing daily in the school of one Tyrannus.

10 And this continued by the space of two years; so that all they which dwelt in Asia heard the word of the Lord Jesus, both Jews and Greeks.

Reading verse 9, we can see Paul in a Bible school — the school of Tyrannus — preaching the Word of God on a daily basis. The result was that within two years, all of Asia Minor had heard the Word of God (v. 10).

It is not likely that all of Asia Minor heard the Word in two years' time because Paul himself preached it. Verse 9 says Paul daily ministered in the Bible school. I believe the students of the Bible school of Tyrannus got fired up and went back to their own countries, home towns, families, and friends and began preaching the Gospel. What happened as a result? Within two years, all of Asia Minor had heard the Gospel!

That's the way we conduct our missions works. We train national missions works to be self-governing, self-supporting, and self-propagating. American missionaries overseas need to learn to trust the nationals and to delegate responsibility.

A missionary can have evangelistic crusades, but if there is no follow-up, there will be no lasting impact. But we want to do something of eternal value for the Kingdom of God in Colombia so that the fruit will remain, and we believe training nationals is the way to do it.

Bible Schools

We started our interdenominational Bible school in Bogotá, holding classes on Saturdays so it would be easy for most people to attend. Many people have to work during the week, and night classes are difficult for many due to the heavy traffic problem.

After we started the Bible school, we started extension schools. An extension school is a mobile Bible school that goes to different cities to help pastors of small churches prepare their people for leadership. Through the extension schools, classes are taught that are similar to the classes in the Bible schools, only not as extensive.

Extension schools are a great benefit to the local pastors who participate. The graduates of these extension schools become the pastors' greatest help in the ministry. Often, the pastors themselves attend the extension schools.

We try to make the Bible school as inexpensive as possible. Our students pay about seven dollars per month, including books. We work with those who cannot afford that by giving them a discount according to their income and circumstances.

All those who receive the discount are expected to help clean up the building after the meetings. There is a half-hour break on class days during which refreshments may be purchased in the cafeteria, which we set up specifically for the occasion. The profits from the cafeteria help to run the Bible school, including helping with students' tuition.

The nationals who teach receive a love offering at the end of the class series if they are not already paid staff members. The missionaries receive their support from the States. We have found this to be effective for us, and we are now in our seventh year of ministry in the Bible schools.

Our goal is to cover Colombia with God's Word! With that in mind, our students are given outlines of their classes at the end of the school year, making it easier for them to teach the same classes to others. We wait until the end of the year to distribute the outlines so the students will take their own notes during the year to study for their tests. We also have plans to expand our Bible school in Bogotá to a full-time Bible school as soon as our new facility is built.

The Vision

Our vision is to maintain and increase outreaches in four areas: (1) our local church; (2) our Bible schools; (3) Mission Colombia, which sponsors seminars and evangelistic crusades; and (4) missions trips.

In our local church, the Church of Colombia, we presently have more than 250 active members who are growing in grace and in the knowledge of God's Word. The church has a ministerial association and sponsors a daily radio program that can be heard throughout the city.

We have several Bible school extensions throughout Colombia. Through these schools, we are raising up qualified leaders in the Body of Christ. These leaders are well-equipped to teach and preach the Gospel of Jesus Christ in their various cities, towns, and villages, and even other nations. We have graduated more than 1,200 students from these schools.

Our ministry, Mission Colombia, sponsors seminars and evangelistic crusades. These seminars have been an effective tool used by God to promote the Bible schools in different parts of Colombia and to focus on extensive Bible teachings, which are commonly confirmed by signs following.

Through seminars and crusades, we have seen hundreds of people ushered from the power of darkness into the Kingdom of God. Those, along with many other believers, become stirred to know more about the life-transforming power of God's Word.

Missions trips are also a part of what we are doing here at Mission Colombia. These missions trips help believers "to look on the fields," which are already white unto harvest (John 4:35). Those who participate are able to experience different aspects of the ministry, including street witnessing, helping in the church, and praying for people at campaigns. They obtain a broader perspective of foreign missions, and it is a life-changing experience for all involved.

My Own Call

Before I attended RHEMA Bible Training Center, the Lord had spoken to me during my prayer time to "go South." During my time at RHEMA, the Lord put South America on my heart, and I began to pray for it on a continual basis. After directing me to go to Guatemala for training, the Lord spoke to my heart to go to Bogotá, Colombia. My wife, whom I met in Guatemala, and I left Guatemala in the Lord's timing.

Learning the Language

The importance of learning a language makes it a priority. You can double your effectiveness and eliminate much frustration by concentrating on learning the language as quickly as possible. This will take time and dedication, and the sooner you begin, the better it will be for you *and* for those to whom you are ministering!

Becoming fluent in the language is not a suggestion; it is a *must* for long-term missions if you plan to be truly effective on the field. We recommend that for the first six months to one year, you spend 50 percent of your workday studying the language.

Many people have a wrong concept in this area. Some think that God will just give them the language supernaturally. That notion is *wrong*! God will help you — the Holy Spirit will bring what you have learned to your remembrance — but *you* must be diligent to study and to prepare.

Second Timothy 2:15 says, *"Study to shew thyself approved unto God, a workman that needeth not to be ashamed, rightly dividing the word of truth."* If we must study to show ourselves approved unto God in the area of God's Word, what makes us think that He would "give" us a language without studying?

Certainly, I understand that at various times, the Spirit of God can give us a message in other tongues. The 120 people in the Upper Room spoke supernaturally; each of those around them heard them speak in his own native language. But these things don't happen on a daily basis, and when they do, they are as *the Spirit* wills and not as *we* will (1 Cor. 12:11).

The younger you are when you start studying a new language, the easier it will be for you. For example, children learn to speak a new language at an incredibly fast rate when they are surrounded by others who speak the language. And a young person 15 to 20 years of age can learn a language and be fluent in only six months. Someone who is 20 to 25 years of age can learn and be fluent in just one year's time.

Those who are ages 25 to 30 usually take an average of two years to become fluent in a new language. Those who are ages 30 to 35 usually take about three years. For every five years in age, the time it generally takes to learn and be fluent in a new language increases by one year.

The missionary's goal is to become fluent enough in the new language to preach and teach without an interpreter. So my recommendation is to begin to learn the language as soon as possible, keeping in mind that the younger you are when you begin, the easier for you it will be.

Culture Shock

Culture shock is natural and is to be expected when moving to a new country. Some people seem to experience it more than others, but all of us can expect to experience it to some degree. It helps to be able to identify it, realize that it is normal, and understand that you are not alone.

I read a book called *Great Commission Handbook (How To Build an Anti-Shock Kit)* that listed four "phases" to adjusting to a new country and new culture. During *phase one*, you are still a tourist. You go to a new country, and it's romantic; everything seems quaint. Your new country is ever so interesting! The euphoria of your experience blurs the cultural differences.

In *phase two*, your new culture no longer seems fascinating. You become very frustrated with the differences; in fact, they can loom so large that they seem intolerable. Feelings of anger, irritation, and helplessness, along with fatigue, produce the classic symptoms of culture shock.

Phase three is a recovery period. Local ideas, events, and practices don't seem so strange anymore. Self-confidence returns, and the negative feelings begin to be replaced with positive ones.

Phase four is *acceptance*. Differences are understood and expected. Your sense of humor returns and you relax more. You're now the "expert," ready to share your hard-earned advice with newcomers (only they won't be quite ready to hear you, because they'll still be in *phase one*!).

When you first move to a foreign country, you will have to rely on others for everything you want to do. You will be learning much new information, and the sooner you learn, the better off you will be. Learners ask "who," "what," "when," "where," and "why" over and over again. Don't be embarrassed to ask questions, for this will help you adjust more easily to your new culture.

Learn to flow with the culture where you are. Put the idea out of your mind that your previous culture is superior. Begin to look at your new culture as merely *different*.

A simple example of a cultural difference here in Colombia is that Colombians don't as a rule mix sweet-tasting ingredients with other sweets in their eating and drinking. For example, they don't put marshmallows in their hot chocolate like Americans do; instead, they put cheese in their hot chocolate! It is perfectly "normal" for an American to put marshmallows in his hot chocolate, but for a Colombian, it would be considered very abnormal. Is one way better than the other? No, it is simply a difference in culture.

If you have a superior attitude, not many will want to hear what you have to say. Learn to be "a Jew to the Jews, and a Greek to the Greeks" (1 Cor. 9:20 and 22). You will find that if you do, people will be much more receptive to you.

Another potential difference in culture that you'll encounter has to do with punctuality. Many other countries do not consider punctuality a virtue. In fact, they don't consider punctuality at all! It is a foreign concept to them. For many, getting a task accomplished the day it was planned is a major accomplishment.

Here in Colombia, arriving late is culturally acceptable and is often seen as a sign that one is important. On the other hand, it is not acceptable or polite to enter the presence of others in a room without greeting each one individually. When saying good-bye, it is proper to go to each one and either shake his or her hand or kiss him or her on the cheek. For this reason, many times Americans are seen as rude, when what it really amounts to are cultural differences.

It is important to learn to adapt to the culture wherever you go and to do it without being critical.

Newsletters

We have found that sending a quarterly newsletter with photos to everyone on our mailing list works well for us. Then once a month, we send a letter of thanks to each supporter with an update of the month's events. This drastically cuts printing and mailing expenses yet still allows supporters to be informed on a monthly basis.

We have also found that with a little experience, we could produce a very good-quality newsletter on a computer using a scanner for the photos and a graphics program for the computer. A laser printer is necessary to obtain the best results.

By producing quality copies of the original, we can cut down on the wear-and-tear on our computer and cut down on the cost of toner, because both photos and graphics use a lot of toner. In this way, we can be good stewards of what the Lord has provided and keep our supporters informed in an economical way.

Itinerating

We have found that some missionaries spend more time itinerating than they do on the field. We don't feel this should be necessary. We spend at least one month per year itinerating, and we trust God to do the rest. Ministering in the churches that support us has been a good way to maintain a solid relationship with them and has added extra financial blessing.

We try to minister in new churches as the Lord opens the doors. We have discovered that months of itineration is not necessary unless one is starting a new work. Our advice to missionaries is to trust the Lord. And to new missionaries, we encourage you not to despise the day of small beginnings. Financial hardship and obstacles are not unusual in the beginning of ministry overseas. We have found that the blessings of God are accumulative, and that prosperity is a process.

Economics

In order to ensure a self-supporting work, we believe it is a wrong assumption that the work must have stateside funds (or funds from other nations) in order to be maintained. If that were the case, then what would happen if the missionary who started the work gets called by God to another country or to start another work in the same country? If the work the missionary has already started is not self-supporting, it will collapse, and there will be no remaining fruit.

Another drawback of allowing a work to depend on finances from the outside is that the people become dependent on outside help and begin to look to the missionary and the outside help as their source instead of looking to God.

Presently, the budget for our work in Colombia, which includes rent, utilities, finances to operate the extension schools, salaries for staff members (nationals), and so forth, comes entirely from Colombia. The work is completely self-supporting, which was our goal from the beginning.

Ninety percent of our building program has been funded by our church members themselves, and we are building on a cash basis. The project will cost $320,000. That is perhaps not much in U.S. dollars, but in a third-world country where the minimum wage is .77 cents per hour, it is a huge amount. But God will supply it, and not just through outside sources!

Some missionaries have the idea that some people are too poor to give anything. Yet we have seen people blessed and prospered by God as they simply gave of what they had. We believe the church should be built by its *members*.

Projects and fund-raisers are good methods of bringing greater unity to the church as they all work together to accomplish the goal. We believe in teaching our people to give and then giving them the opportunity to do so without putting pressure on them. Then as God prospers them for their faith and obedience, they learn for *themselves* the blessing of sowing and reaping. To paraphrase an old saying, "If you give a man a fish, he will have a meal; but if you teach a man to fish, he can eat every day of his life."

Missionary Lifestyle

The person who desires to become a missionary should essentially be faithful in a local church and submitted to a pastor. Faithfulness is a very important key to a person's success on the mission field. For example, if you have not been a blessing in your own country, you will not be a blessing in another country.

Your pastor should be sad to see you leave because of the help you have been to him and the local church. But if you have not been a servant in your own church and in your own country, simply crossing the border will not change you. Those who are faithful and who are a blessing at home will be the same on the mission field. In other words, those who are faithful in little will also be faithful in much (Luke 19:17).

A well-developed prayer life and good study habits are also essential if you expect to have something to give to the people spiritually. These habits should be developed before you go to the field. Living waters do not flow from a person who is not filled. They may trickle, but you need more than a *trickle* to impact the hearts of people.

It is also important to make friends and have fellowship with the people once you arrive on the field. It is necessary to have close contact with the people so that you can better know and minister to their needs.

Jesus was known as a friend to sinners and publicans. And, likewise, we need to listen to the hearts of the people to whom we are ministering and learn about them. We should not just be known as someone who simply ministers from the pulpit, someone who comes to give money or hand-outs, someone who shows movies, or someone who provides medical services.

A missionary's lifestyle should not be one of much luxury. For example, if the nationals see you eating in restaurants where the check is more than they earn in a week, it will probably put a big gap between you and them. They may begin to see you as the "rich gringos" and may not be able to relate to you.

They may also begin asking you for financial help. We are trying to teach the nationals to make God their source, not us.

Legal Aspects

We recommend that you investigate the current laws of the country where God has called you. We also encourage you to stay abreast of changes, especially when there is a change of government or changes in administration.

Try to do everything according to the law as much as possible (the only exception to this is when it is against the law to preach the Gospel). Be patient with the legalities. Most countries outside of the U.S. are extremely slow with paperwork, and sometimes it takes years to get things accomplished.

If at all possible, have your accountant do your bookkeeping within the country where you are ministering and set up your ministry board within the country. We are not incorporated in the United States, but we are incorporated in Colombia. We have been very blessed to have RHEMA Bible Church handle our stateside finances, so there has been no need to incorporate stateside.

Are You Truly Called?

How will you know if you are really called to missions? Here at Mission Colombia, we do not accept anyone to come and work with us unless they first come on a short-term missions trip.

Spying out the land is scriptural. For example, Moses sent the children of Israel into Canaan land to spy it out before they went in to possess it (Num. 13:17). Many times, God confirms the call during a person's short-term missions trip.

After taking a short-term trip, the person who is truly called to that particular mission will want to return in spite of the hardships he may have experienced, such as: lack of hot water (or lack of any water at all at times!), problems with pollution, and seemingly never-ending traffic jams. Those are some of the things one may experience here in Bogotá.

The person with a call has the grace to endure hardships when he is confronted with them. His focus is on the harvest, not on the hardship.

Many people have a desire to go to the foreign field, but very often their motives are wrong. The adventure of traveling to a faraway land, sleeping in a mud hut, or experiencing an exotic culture is alluring.

But are they willing to endure the everyday hardships that almost always come in one form or another on the mission field? Is compassion the motivating force that compels them? A person needs to be honest with himself and with God. If his motivation is wrong, he won't make it; he will not endure when his faith is tried by fire.

The excitement and adventure of a missions trip can sometimes cause people to think that God is calling them to the mission field. We recommend that after a candidate travels short-term to the mission field, he should return home and begin to pray consistently about God's will. If after at least several months of prayer, the desire is still present and he has the inner witness or has heard the Voice of the Lord, it is safe to say that he is not making a decision based on an emotional experience.

We believe that having the assurance in your heart that God has called you is vitally important. When the trials and difficulties come, it's easy to throw in the towel if you are not absolutely sure you've heard from God and that you are in the right place at the right time.

More on Short-Term Missions Trips

We have found that short-term missions trips are a vision-broadening experience for all who participate. These trips give people the opportunity to be laborers in the harvest as well as firsthand experience on the mission field. Participants are involved in various aspects of the ministry — from the helps ministry and preaching in the streets to praying for the needs of the people during the campaigns.

As I said, God often confirms a missionary call upon people's lives during these kinds of trips. And many times, after visiting the field, even those who discover they are not called to missions become more active in missions through their giving.

Some Final Thoughts

In missions as well as any other ministry, we should concentrate on building the Kingdom of God and not our own kingdom. We should not be concerned with our "image" or with trying to promote ourselves or our own ministry.

When missionaries try to promote their own image, their newsletters often become more fiction than fact. Then they begin to minister to people, not for the *people's* benefit, but for their *own* so they will have something to report back to the States.

We need to maintain our love for the Lord and our love for the people at all times. Success is doing what God told you to do, not what other people think you should do. Don't be moved by what people perceive of you or your ministry or by what they expect of you. Always keep your heart pure, and you will be a blessing to many!

Chapter 7
Called to Preparation

By Jim Andrews ('79 '80)

After graduating from RHEMA, Jim ('79 '80) and Faye Andrews, spent three years in Guatemala working with an established ministry. In 1984, they moved to establish a new work in Lima, Peru. Besides the Bible school in Lima, the Andrews have pioneered a church in that city and have started satellite churches and Bible schools throughout the nation of Peru. The Andrews also minister throughout Peru with evangelistic campaigns and have hosted several short-term missions trips made to Peru by RHEMA Bible Training Center students and members of various churches in the States.

After Faye and I received the Lord Jesus Christ in 1975, we began to listen to Rev. Kenneth E. Hagin's teachings. Then we learned about Kenneth Hagin Ministries' Campmeeting and attended our first one in 1976. It was there at Campmeeting that we were moved upon by the Holy Spirit to attend RHEMA Bible Training Center.

For us, like many, the decision to attend RHEMA Bible Training Center was a major one. But, thank God, we made the right decision and attended RHEMA!

We thank God for RHEMA and for the spirit of faith that was "imparted" to us there. When we later moved to Guatemala as missionaries, our daughter became very sick with a fever, and had it not been for the Word that was put into us at RHEMA, I believe our daughter would have died.

Following the Lord's Leading

Being called into missions was something I didn't seriously think about or consider until our first year at RHEMA. But now I can see that the call to missions was working in me from the time we received the Lord. For example, many times when missionaries would come to our church to speak, my heart would be stirred toward missions. At one time, I even asked one of the leaders of our denomination what he thought about me going to the mission field. He discouraged me, telling me that by the time I received the necessary training to prepare me, I would be too old to go!

I was 30 years old at that time with four children. Today we are in our fourteenth year on the field as missionaries!

During our first year at RHEMA, my heart began to be stirred again toward missions. I thought surely that we would be going to Africa. After all, that's what missions meant to me — *Africa, living in a mud hut*!

We thank God that we did not go to the foreign field in haste, as we still needed to avail ourselves of the second-year program at RHEMA. We have learned that days of preparation are never wasted days. The truth is, what we learned during our second year at RHEMA is probably what saved our daughter's life.

How It All Began for Us

I know that there are different ways the Holy Spirit leads people, but I am going to share about the way the Lord led *us*.

Looking back over my life, I realize that deep down, I've always thought about going to another country to live. Like many, however, I had never even been to a foreign country.

After our graduation from RHEMA, an opportunity arose for me to go to Guatemala. We decided that I would go, not really praying about it, just sensing that it was the right thing to do. The Lord ministered to me in a special way on that trip, even though I was sick for about three days.

Once I was back in the States, I saw the need, but did not sense the leading of the Lord to return to Guatemala. Then in January 1981, after continually seeking the Lord and working faithfully in a local church, the Lord spoke to me at a prayer breakfast I was attending. He spoke in a very audible, authoritative Voice for us to go to Guatemala!

When I received that direction from the Lord, I tried in a roundabout sort of way to see what direction my wife had received. Eventually, we discovered that we *both* knew it was the Lord's will that we move to Guatemala.

We called a family meeting and announced to our children our decision to move to Guatemala. To our surprise, the Lord had already dealt with them! We never had a moment's trouble with our children regarding the missionary call.

All this happened in January 1981. It took us a month to follow through on commitments with our employers. We didn't want to stain or taint the image of RHEMA in their eyes by being unfaithful.

It took us two months to actually arrive on the field. I sensed an urgency to get to the field at that time, so after we received approval from the mission with which we would work in Guatemala, we moved quickly to get to the field.

Getting to the Field

Many new missionaries have to fight the "tin-cup" image that they're begging for money. Missionaries must do their part and share their vision and raise support. But they need the support of the local church. In the beginning, all of a missionary's support comes from abroad — from a country other than the one in which he is living and ministering.

In most countries, a missionary is not allowed to work in that country because if he was allowed to work, he might be taking a job away from a national who could fill the position. In many cases, even if the missionary did work, the pay scale would be so low that his salary would not be enough to make a difference — to help him live and minister in that country.

Probably the greatest challenge for new missionaries is the raising of support. I actually read a book in which a man said that the day of the Western missionary was over and that churches should only support national ministers! But God still calls "Western" missionaries, and He has enough supply and provision to send those whom He calls!

Even though a missionary is called, the financial challenge is still present. The problem that the new missionary faces is that of credibility, as he probably hasn't done anything ministry-wise to establish himself and to merit the confidence of others.

That's one reason I suggest that people be faithful in the local church and put their hands to the plow, so to speak, wherever they are and in whatever capacity. New missionaries need a base of support in the local church.

When we went to Guatemala, there were only a few Word churches, and it took some time to build up our finances. The mission we worked with in Guatemala wanted us to come and offered to help us with our finances. We had very little, and it took us three months to get furniture for our house. During that time, our children slept on cots (and never complained).

The Voice of Experience

Everyone who is called to be a missionary should go to the field for a visit or for a short-term trip.

There are two primary reasons for this: First, he should go to confirm his call. If the would-be missionary is married, his spouse should go too. Wives need to see the country they are called to *before* they arrive on the field to live! Women are simply more practical than men, and seeing the country will eliminate many of the concerns they may have as homemakers and especially as mothers.

Second, the person with a call to missions should make a short-term visit to the field first because he needs the *experience*. That experience combined with his confidence in his calling will enable him to speak with conviction about going to the field.

Most people are not moved to give or to help you financially just because you want to go try out something! But if you speak about your calling from your heart *with conviction*, they will generally hook up with you.

Ways To Maintain Contact With Your Supporters

The new missionary must make contact with the local churches. I believe this is the plan of God to bless the local church. When a church gives to missions, they are really giving in faith because they can't see firsthand where the money goes unless they visit the field themselves. The missionary's contact with the church will be the link between them and the mission field and will inspire them in their desire to support mission works.

By all means, have a newsletter. However, visual contacts speak louder than letters, so try to make personal contact with your supporters before you go onto the field and when you are back in the States after you've already moved to the field.

When making personal contacts, here are a few things to remember: Pastors are busy, so if you do get to meet the pastor, be mindful of his time. What you don't respect, you will eventually lose. Don't be ignorant of the fact that the pastor also has a vision and a call to fulfill. You must be willing to help him in his vision and call. His goal is to prepare people for ministry whether as laypersons or as full-time ministers, and some will go to the mission field!

When you meet with a pastor, always leave something in his hands about your ministry to meditate on and review. Your newsletter should be simple, easy to read, and informative. It should inform readers about the country to which you will go, what you will do, your projected date of departure if you are a new missionary, and where and how your money will be handled.

There are several ways to handle your finances. You could have your finances handled through your local church if that service is available. The local church can be a great blessing to you in your missionary venture.

For RHEMA graduates who are members of the RHEMA Ministerial Association International, RHEMA offers these services. RHEMA graduates should contact the RMAI office for a list of requirements and other necessary information.

Buying, Packing, and Shipping

As elementary as it may seem, the missionary must get his things to the field, and there are right and wrong ways to go about doing that! For example, don't buy expensive luggage; international travel is rough on luggage. Buy something light, as 70 pounds per person is normally the limit you may take on a plane. Locks are a must, and even then, valuables should not be put in your luggage but in your carry-on bags.

Shipping could be the way to transport your belongings. However, information on customs, taxes, and so forth should be acquired before shipping. Always insure what you ship.

When you buy clothes to take abroad, buy them with quality in mind because in many countries, the water and the detergent are very hard on clothes. When packing new clothes, always take the price tags off and wash the clothes if possible. Some countries will tax you on a certain amount of new clothes you bring into the country, especially if you have a resident visa.

First Things First

There are several things that must be done when you first get to the country where you will be ministering.

First, establish your home base. Singles have it easier than families in this respect, as they can live in the house of a national for a while, which will also facilitate the learning of the native tongue. (Regardless of whether you're single or married, the native language must be learned!)

Second, once you are located in your new country, bank accounts should be opened. Birth certificates, marriage certificates, and other legal documents must be taken with you to the country — originals, not copies.

Money Is Very Important

It is also necessary to bring adequate finances with you to set up housing and ministry facilities. The amount will depend on how you plan to receive your finances in the country. Remember, it could take a long time to receive money from the States. Housing in another country could cost you up to a year's rent *in advance*.

The best way we have found to handle our finances is to have our money deposited in our stateside account. Then we can deposit or transfer the money into the country where we are living. But I have a word of caution for you: Be careful how much money you keep on hand in banks in foreign countries. In the last 10 years in Peru, we have had three currency changes, and several times, all bank accounts were frozen.

Language, Not Tongues

I have heard stories about the gift of spontaneously being able to communicate in another language by a manifestation of the Holy Spirit. But that doesn't happen most of the time. For the missionary to be effective on a long-term basis, he simply must learn the language of the country in which he is ministering.

I am by no means making light of praying in tongues, as praying in the Spirit in other tongues is one of the best ways to pray and build yourself up spiritually. But I'm talking about language — the language of a country — not tongues.

The learning of another language and the ability to preach from the heart in that language rather than reading your sermon will come after study and the discipline to practice what you study. When we arrived in Peru, we forgot about English and dove into Spanish, the language of the people. I read very little in English and almost never read my English Bible.

Keep the Vision Alive and Cast Not Away Your Confidence

The Bible says that without a vision the people perish (Prov. 29:18). That applies to you too!

A vision, a goal, for your life and ministry will keep your soul anchored. I believe that in starting any new work, the greatest danger is in the "infant" stage of the work. It is during this stage that it's easiest to become discouraged. You must keep the vision before you, even if it's not specific.

For us, just getting to the field in Guatemala and setting up our ministry pushed us past the difficulties we experienced in raising support. Then on the way to Peru, where we now minister, a more specific vision began to develop, which involved three things. The Lord didn't speak in an audible Voice; it just seemed to come into my heart to do these three things: 1) raise up a strong church in the capital city of Lima; 2) conduct Bible seminars for pastors and leaders, teaching them the Word; and 3) raise up a Bible training center.

The Birthing of a Church

In fulfilling our vision, we started off slowly. Through a series of events, we began holding meetings in our home, where we ministered healing to many.

We had already taught in several Bible studies, and the people began to call us "pastor." We never told them that we were going to raise up a church.

We began holding meetings in our home, teaching on Thursday nights. After about a month, we decided to start teaching on Sunday mornings. The Lord spoke to us that these would be miracle services.

(We were not located on the poor side of town, but on the side of town where the upper-class live. We have learned that the people will graduate upward better than downward. The social classes are very prevalent in Peru.)

In the first Sunday morning miracle service in our house, legs grew out, a blind man received his sight, and the deaf were instantly healed. From that time, what happened in the country of Peru is difficult to explain. People began to come from everywhere! To say the least, we were not prepared for it! Our house filled up, the patio filled up, and people would come and stand for hours!

Then we moved to an abandoned movie theater. The first morning we were there, the church doubled in size. Literally hundreds of people were coming to the Lord. I believe that now, after 10 years, we are prepared for such a thing, but at that time, we were not.

A new pastor should develop leaders; that's the only way to handle growth. Much of our permanent growth came from other churches, although it wasn't our intention to have people come from other churches to our church. People who hunger for God will be filled. That's why they became a permanent part of our church; they wanted more of the Word.

Looking back over the first five years of our church's existence, I see that we functioned mainly as a revival center. But we have learned that evolution is a must if a church is to survive. In other words, the work must evolve to become a bona fide local church.

A local church is a family, and it is a place where ministry is provided for the whole man and for the whole family. From 1986 through 1990, 8,000 new people came to the altars at the church in Lima. We managed to maintain only a very small percentage of these in our church because as I said, we simply weren't prepared for such a revival.

Maintaining Good Relations With National Ministers

There is a saying, "People don't care how much you *know* until they know how much you *care*." If you are going to minister to ministers on the field, you must learn to relate to them in their setting. Outside of Lima we had no problems in this respect, but in Lima it was another story.

We didn't have much trouble with other pastors until we started a church — one that was growing rapidly. Then we began to have some problems. For example, hundreds of people from different denominations were receiving the Holy Spirit because of our ministry, and this caused us problems with the national pastors. The fear of losing people in their church is one of the greatest obstacles with the national pastor. However, if you develop a relationship with them, it will be easier.

As a missionary, you must learn how to deal with rejection because not everybody will welcome your arrival in another country.

Ministering to ministers or pastors is different than ministering to laypeople. My particular calling is to preach and teach and help the local church develop spiritually. I understand my calling and the practical aspects of fulfilling it better today than at the beginning.

I say this because missionaries can destroy their relationships with national pastors if they are overzealous in developing the pastors or are too quick to give handouts.

For example, it's easy to present the great "white father" image instead of simply giving people the Word. But give the Word first and then help those who really take hold of the Word. Then you will not be building for the Kingdom in vain.

Finances are one of the major problems between missionaries and national pastors, and there have been abuses in the area of finances on both sides.

In dealing with national pastors, what you commit to do, *do it*! Remember, what you do with consistency will produce better results. So keep your word. If you don't, your credibility will be lost. Once you lose respect as a minister, you will lose your effectiveness in teaching the Word of God.

Write down all of your agreements. This will avoid much confusion and offense with nationals. A word of caution for stateside pastors: Don't make promises to nationals. Always deal through the missionary because if you've dealt directly with the national, then when you leave the area or the country, the missionary will have to make good your promise in order to maintain his integrity in the country.

Training of Nationals Is a Must

To be able to affect a permanent change in a country, the Gospel must get to the people. They must be trained not only in the Word but also in the things of the Spirit. You must answer the "when," "where," "how," and "who" of accomplishing this task. Different areas of a country require different methods of ministry.

We decided from the beginning to videotape all of our classes. Video cameras, whether they be super-8 mm or VHS cameras, are not expensive, and the quality has improved greatly. Because of the size of the country and the economy, it is virtually impossible for many to travel to Lima to study. That's why the video Bible schools have been such a blessing. We now have four schools and plan to open five more in the near future. With the videos, it's easy to set up the schools almost anywhere, and it is very cost-effective.

However, this kind of teaching must be followed up by "live," in-person teaching with a demonstration of the Holy Spirit. I can't overemphasize the importance of a missionary demonstrating the operation of the Spirit.

Study materials are of premium value. We put Rev. Kenneth E. Hagin and Rev. Kenneth Hagin Jr.'s books into the hands of the national pastors. Remember, you train in different ways, and in one sense, everything you do is training, be it good or bad.

'I'd Rather Burn Out Than Rust Out'?

You probably have heard that saying before, but I say you don't have to do either! You don't have to burn out *or* rust out! You can finish your course *and* keep your health and sanity while you do it!

There is a tendency in ministry to have the "savior syndrome" and a "must-do-it-all" attitude. While diligence is necessary on the mission field, you cannot do it all.

The missionary faces some unique challenges on the field. He is his own boss, separated by land or sea from his supporters. Just getting to the field has demanded a great degree of personal motivation, and normally the missionary is a motivated person. He or she lives in a foreign land, speaks a different language, and the cultural differences are many.

Because of the desire to reach out, missionaries often operate on "go" all the time. He is presented with needs all the time. For example, when he goes to the store, there may be 10 or 15 children or adults there begging. It could be a normal everyday occurrence so that no matter where he goes, the needs of the poor and disabled are with him constantly.

The missionary must take time to rest. He must also take time with his family. And it's a *must* that the missionary maintain a life in the Word and prayer. Many have asked me how I stay built up. I've always relied on prayer and the Word.

The missionary should always have time to rest, eat right, keep his body in shape, and play or enjoy times of recreation. I also believe a missionary should have a good, comfortable home.

Missionaries should not return to the States burned out. Remember, when your outgo becomes more than your income, your upkeep will be your downfall. So when you return to the States, schedule some time just to fellowship around the Word with those of your own company. As RHEMA graduates, we stay hooked up with RHEMA and its events and activities. We know from whence we came, what we have been taught at RHEMA, and the testimony that we have as a result. Therefore, we choose to remain united with our spiritual roots at RHEMA.

Enlarging Your Circle

As your work grows, you will continually be faced with change. Not all of it is good. We have experienced this many times on the field. We were sued more than nine times, our car has been impounded, and warrants for our arrest were issued on three different occasions.

We have also faced persecutions from brothers in the Lord. And the legal system in other countries is not like the legal system in the States. In many foreign countries, the asking of "bribes" is a common occurrence, and many times, it is better for you to have a bad "agreement" than a good case in court.

Satan is a master at diversion to keep you off-focus. Diluted expertise is when you are diverted from your primary call. So avoid court cases — they consume your time, your money, and your peace!

In order to enlarge your circle, you must enlarge your foundations — your financial as well as physical resources. Time-management is a must. And as the saying goes, the only way to get more time is to use somebody else's. Delegation is a big factor in time-management.

For the missionary, because the bulk of ministry is paid by funding from the States, he is required to travel more to make his vision known to the people. But as the local churches grow in the States, they could also grow in their support of missions, thereby making it easier for the missionary to be more effective on the field.

As a missionary, don't get in a hurry, and don't go beyond your financial abilities. Excess financial pressures have been the destruction of many good works. But no matter how large or successful your ministry becomes, if you don't take the time to be enlarged spiritually by the Lord and His Word, enlargement in any other area of your life or ministry will be difficult to hold on to. In other words, enlargement begins with *you*. Your ministry will only be as successful as your ministry to the Lord and your relationship with Him. Then you can trust Him to enlarge your circle of ministry and prosper the work of your hands.

Chapter 8
Team Ministry Overseas: Sharing the Living Word Through Living Word Training Center

By Carol Leaphart ('89 '90)

In November 1990, Carol Leaphart moved to the Philippines to work with Living Word Training Center. Before becoming a missionary, she attended RHEMA Bible Training Center in Broken Arrow, Oklahoma, graduating in May 1990. She was employed at RHEMA Bible Church while she was a student at RHEMA. She also served as a volunteer worker in Children's Church, the Prayer and Healing Center as a phone counselor, the RHEMA Bible Church Bookstore, and with the altar care-team.

Carol is the director of Living Word Training Center. She teaches in the training center and conducts pastors' seminars and ministers' meetings throughout the Philippines.

Carol has three children: Bernard Leaphart and his wife Jeanine; April Thrusten and her husband Charles; and Terri, her youngest daughter. Carol also has two grandchildren: Joya, age three, and Samuel, who is ten months old.

I had wanted to be a missionary since I was 12 years old, but life's circumstances, including the raising of three children as a widow, postponed the call for 30 years.

So what do you do if you know you're called to the mission field, but you're a female past 40 years of age and single? First, be confident of your calling. From the earliest beginnings of world evangelism, women have been called, anointed, and greatly used by God.

Married female missionaries have served faithfully beside their husbands on countless foreign fields. These very special women successfully raised their children in the face of tremendous challenges and sometimes adverse circumstances.

Often, the single female missionary is another breed of missionary altogether. I am privileged to tell you *my* story:

How I *Knew* I Was Called to Missions

While I was completing my second year at RHEMA Bible Training Center, I was given an opportunity to participate in a 10-day missions trip to the Philippines. Part of the preparation for that trip, aside from raising the money to go, was joining a special prayer group that prayed for the trip months in advance.

This prayer group was started by the Prayer and Healing Center at RHEMA. During one of those prayer sessions, I saw in a vision a strange group of people surrounded by darkness. They were neither black nor white. While they sat in darkness, they did not complain; it was as if they didn't even know or realize that darkness was engulfing them. They were just "existing." The lifelessness and lack of purpose in their eyes pierced my heart. I was greatly moved by what I saw.

Then I heard the Holy Spirit say to me, "I'm sending you to get them out."

During another time of prayer with the prayer group, I saw another vision of an Asian rice farmer standing in the middle of a rice field that was ready to be harvested. He shouted from the center of that field, "Come over here and help us!"

When we arrived in the Philippines for our missions trip, the people looked just like the people I had in my heart — those I'd seen in the vision. What I saw and experienced on that ministry visit changed my life; I have never been the same.

There's *Grace* in the *Going*

Once I made the decision that it was the will of God for me to be a missionary in the Philippines, I then needed to choose a location in that country. Those early days of pursuing the call were spent mostly in prayer and listening to what the Holy Spirit was saying to my spirit.

I sensed that I was on the right track concerning the Philippines; I had no question about the nation to which I was to go. However, I did need to be able to articulate the *method* God had chosen for me to bring the message to that nation.

In other words, would I go alone and pioneer a missions station? Or would I join a mission team that was already established?

I had heard many of the advantages of starting your own missions station: You would be your own director; there would be no conflict of vision or purpose; it would be easier to raise support. However, I also learned that you could become more effective *sooner* on the mission field if you joined an already existing missions team.

After considering these factors, I elected to become a part of a team ministry in a remote area of the Philippines.

Team Ministry on the Field

Once I decided to join a team, I knew it would be with the ministry team we had visited on our short-term missions trip. Part of their ministry, Keys to Freedom Ministries, was in a remote area of the Philippines called Catbalogan Samar.

Paul Chase and his wife, Shoddy, are the founders of that ministry. They are also graduates of RHEMA Bible Training Center. My first step was to contact their stateside office to inquire if they would even consider me as a member of their ministry team.

It is always better to contact a missionary's stateside office for inquires such as this; office personnel can answer your questions more quickly. After contacting the Chases' office, an application was sent to my home. It was about five pages long. I was intimidated by so many questions about my personal life and questions about what God was speaking to my heart and what areas of ministry I felt He was leading me to.

On the Keys to Freedom application was a list of every one of their ministry outreaches. Just reading the list thrilled and inspired me: *Evangelistic Boat Ministry*; *Living Word Bible Training Center*; *God's Lambs* (a feeding center for malnourished children); *Lighthouse* (a youth outreach); *Crusade Ministry*; *Hospital Ministry;* and *Local Church Ministry.*

I was in "missionary heaven" just reading the application! Then I had to choose the areas in which I thought God would use me in their ministry. Filling out that application helped me get a stronger picture on the inside about what God had called me to do.

In the months that followed, while I was waiting to hear from Keys to Freedom Ministries, people would ask me, "What are you going to do there?" I would just say what I saw on the application. I would tell them, "I'm going to teach in the Bible school and in the local churches."

I kept on saying that, and it became real on the inside of me. I believed it! I saw myself teaching those precious Filipino men and women who would be coming from all over the Philippines to be trained to reach their nation with the Gospel.

The Day I Received the News

May 20, 1990, the day after my graduation from RHEMA Bible Training Center, Rev. Paul Chase was holding a missions meeting in Tulsa, Oklahoma. One of Brother Paul's administrators had called me the day before and asked me to attend that meeting. It was there that Brother Paul announced to me, "We want you to join our team in the Philippines."

Then he said, "You'll be teaching in the Bible school in Catbalogan Samar"! It was an "epoch" day for me — one of those days that changed my entire life forever.

Natural Preparations

After hearing the news, I was so excited! My spirit was soaring, but there were things I needed to do in the natural to walk things out further. I knew I was called. I knew the location. I knew how I would minister. But now I needed finances.

How do you get people behind you to support you when you don't have a track record? How do you tell someone, "I'm going somewhere I've only visited before for ten days. It's ten thousand miles away, I'll be doing something I've never done before, and, by the way, I'm going alone. And did I mention, Pastor and Mrs. Big Bucks, that *I'm a woman?*"

In those wonderful preparation days — days of hard-core reality — my precious Shepherd gave me Proverbs 3:5 and 6: *"Trust in the Lord with all thine heart; and lean not unto thine own understanding. In all thy ways acknowledge him, and he shall direct thy paths."*

In essence, the Lord told me, "Trust in Me with all your heart, and do not lean to your own understanding to get you to the mission field."

The very worst thing you can do in your days of preparation and of gathering finances is to depend on what you know to promote you! Instead, trust God; He will not anoint you to go without anointing people to send you.

In November of 1990 I was living in the nation of the Philippines. From the time of my graduation from Bible school in May 1990, I'd had six months to get things in order financially, naturally, and spiritually.

Financial Preparation

I was working at RHEMA Bible Church at the time I knew I would be going to work with Paul and Shoddy Chase. But I had no money in the bank, no one knew me, and I had never preached in a pulpit except during my lab class at the training center.

I was hired at RHEMA Bible Church as a receptionist at the Ninowski Recreation Center. But in light of my newest plans, I asked to be transferred to housekeeping in the Student Housing complex. I just couldn't sit still behind a desk! Something big was on the inside of me, and I felt I needed to get myself in a situation where I could pray, listen to tapes, and feed my faith. So for that entire summer, I cleaned bathrooms and prayed, shampooed carpets and prayed, washed walls and prayed, and cleaned out ovens and prayed some more!

Every day, I believed God for divine appointments. I *had* to — there were no *natural* appointments! Then it began to happen: It seems the favor of God just "came upon me."

One day as I was coming out of one of those apartments with a coworker, a car pulled up in front of us. There we stood, dirty and sweaty in our work uniforms, with mop and bucket in hand. In the car was a pastor who was a RHEMA graduate. He was visiting the RHEMA campus and needed directions.

After giving him the directions he needed, my coworker began telling this pastor what God was sending me to the Philippines to do. The pastor just looked at me and said, "My wife and I have been believing God for a new missionary to support!" That pastor and his church have supported me since 1990.

Other Financial Victories

As a RHEMA employee, I was assigned to work in the Radio Booth during Campmeeting week in 1990. While working, a woman came to the booth, and we began talking. She and her husband pastored a church in Connecticut. Before I knew it, she and her husband had invited me to come speak at their church. They asked me to do a Ministry of Helps seminar. As I said, I had never preached or taught outside of my lab class, but I did have a working understanding of the ministry of helps.

If you have an idea that you're called as a missionary, especially to a third-world country, get involved in all the areas of helps that you possibly can! Do it all; you will need the experience. You might be the only one on the mission field with a point of reference for organizing schools, churches, youth meetings, pastors' seminars, and so forth! So prepare yourself by getting involved in your local church.

As a missionary, you will be the one teaching and training the leaders in that country. They will look to you for practical church-operating wisdom. Before I attended RHEMA, I had worked in various areas of helps in a church in Arizona. I also got involved in several areas of helps at RHEMA Bible Church while I was at the training center studying for the ministry.

When I went to Connecticut to hold the helps seminar, I taught the people for five straight hours on a Saturday with only 10-minute breaks between each session. I was exhausted and could hardly walk when I was finished. But that night, the pastor's wife held up one of my newsletters and said to the congregation, "This weekend, I believe we can get Carol's airfare to the Philippines!" You can just imagine the joy I was experiencing on the inside!

My airfare to the Philippines was $900. The following morning after I delivered the Sunday morning message, the pastor and his wife handed me an envelope with $1,200 in it! But here is the real testimony: There were only 30 people in that church!

Then there was a particular church I was very familiar with that I expected would support me. The pastor let me preach and gave me a love offering, but no monthly support. However, he referred me to a church that turned out to be one of my major church supporters, and they have supported me since 1990.

Then I received two more church referrals from an evangelist and his wife who heard I was going to the Philippines. Those two churches have also supported me since 1990.

The reason I'm sharing all of this is to encourage you not only to seek the Lord about your call, but to seek *the Lord of the call*. He has a financial plan for you. I know personally that God will not only anoint you to *go*, He will also anoint people to *send* you and to stay hooked up with you financially and prayerfully on the mission field.

The Role of Newsletters
In Your Days of Preparation

Give God something to work with. You need to write a letter that clearly states your vision or goals and your plans to accomplish them. Please keep in mind that many people have read these kinds of letters many times before. Ask yourself the following questions: What is special or different about my newsletter? Is it exciting and fresh? Is it easy to read?

If you're not talented at formulating a clear, informative, to-the-point letter, get some help in doing so. To print your newsletter, there are many print shops in America to assist you.

After you've created your newsletter, then position yourself by the Holy Spirit. In other words, go where He tells you to go and see who He tells you to see. "Before-you-go-to-the-field" finances are the very hardest to obtain, but with a true call in your heart and a determination to honor God by fulfilling that call, it can be done.

The Inspiration in Preparation

A missionary has to be the most highly motivated person in the world! This truth echoed in my ears, so to speak, in those months of planning to go to the field. Every day I would set myself to accomplish something. Even if it was a small thing, accomplishing it took me one step closer to my goal.

I once heard a minister say, "*Destiny* is day by day refusing to give up, lay down, or quit."

In pursuing the call of God on your life, your well-meaning friends may tell you, "Stay home with us. You need to put away those dreams and act normal!" But if you are a missionary, there's not a "normal" bone in your body!

A missionary is one of the most unusual of all God's created beings. They're bold, determined, relentless, courageous, instigators, initiators, and they have the audacity to expect nations to change and be transformed because they preach and teach the Gospel of living hope through the resurrection of Jesus Christ from the dead!

Monthly Support and the First Year on the Field

After I arrived in the Philippines, another reality hit me: *Monthly support — I really need it!*

Monthly supporters are a different kind of giver than a one-time-gift giver. As I already stated, I'm convinced that some are called to *go* and some are called to *send*. And there is grace for both.

In my first year on the field, there were days that I just lived by faith in the faithful God. I really don't have any sad stories to tell — only exciting adventures of how God answered prayers while He was inspiring people to support me.

Once during my first year on the field, there was the case of "the triplets." They were born on a nearby island. I had been here about seven months, and people knew me as the American who buys milk for dying babies. So they came to me about these triplets. It seemed that the mother already had five children and for medical reasons was unable to nurse the triplets.

The babies were in very bad shape. I had only $50, the only money I would have for a while, but my Lord inspired someone to send me cash directly to the Philippines! So I was able to help those babies. These types of incidents increased my faith.

During the first two years on the mission field, you'll have a wonderful opportunity to develop solid faith — the kind that new ministry outreaches can later be built upon.

My total budget my first year was $6,000. But I remained steadfast and unmovable in the Lord. And I encourage you, too, to remain steadfast and unmovable no matter how scary things may look on the field, especially during your first year. If you fall down, get back up. Make a determined decision to outlast the difficulty. The glory of God for that nation is at stake. Don't allow circumstances to send you home before your time is up on the field.

Financial Obligation to Your Ministry Team

As much as I can, I want to help you get an on-the-field view of overseas missions. There are many things you can do to prepare yourself spiritually and naturally that will make your transition easier.

If you will be joining a ministry team, one of the things you should know before you go is what your financial obligation will be to the ministry you are joining. Every ministry is different, so just because you know about one overseas ministry doesn't mean you know about them all.

I have missionary friends who have joined other missions teams, and their only obligation is their personal housekeeping expenses, personal ministry expenses, rent, car, and so forth. In that case, the founder of that particular ministry is raising all the finances for that ministry operation.

But other ministries are different. In some cases, you agree to share in the financial responsibilities of that ministry on a monthly basis.

Our ministry is set up that way, and I personally like investing in what I believe in. I see the good, strong fruit we're producing, and I want to have a share in it through my giving.

The Lord has blessed me over the years with great partners who have a vision for Asia and for the Gospel to be implanted in the hearts of the people. Because of my supporters, we are one of the top givers on the team here in Catbalogan. I believe God to increase my finances so I can give more every year. I really believe in the work we're doing in the Philippines.

The Vast Importance of Monthly Support: Educating Your Supporters

As a missionary, part of your job will be to educate your supporters about missions and to communicate with them your vision as well as your ongoing work.

An ongoing work needs ongoing support. What many churches and individual supporters don't realize is that even when they fail to send your support one particular month or stop supporting you completely without notice, you still have a major financial obligation to meet. There are lives at stake.

After a few years on the field, most missionaries hire a staff to work with them. They develop their own ministry outreaches. So if there is a shortage of funds one particular month, the missionary really feels the crunch. Often, he will compensate for the shortage with his own personal funds even if it is at great sacrifice. Ministry is not just a word; ministry is *people*. A missionary would do almost anything before he'd allow the people to whom he is sent to be hurt, go hungry, or be hindered from hearing the Gospel.

Loyalty and Team Ministry: Being Faithful to God, the Call, and the Team

As a missionary, if you choose to work in a team setting, *please* do not choose it because it could be a springboard for your ministry. It takes time to develop you as a missionary. The new culture of a country and the team you work with are God's sculpting tools for shaping you, your character, and your vision. In the natural, it takes two years to earn an associate's degree at a university and four years to earn a bachelor's degree. Why then be in such a hurry to leave a ministry while you're yet being shaped? As you successfully go through every crisis or difficulty, vital dimensions are being added to your character and your walk with God.

When God first called me to Living Word Training Center, He clearly said I was to be here two years. I heard it, and I obeyed it. Obedience to God's known will anchors you through both the good times and the frustrating times.

Near the end of my first two years, I heard God say, "Invest another five years." I was being guided, and I had another anchor.

I can't overemphasize the importance of loyalty to the team with which you minister, to the call, and to the timing of God. Ministry does not come upon us; it comes up *out of* us in due season.

Loyalty to your team and to the call and the timing of God means staying put, even when things seem difficult with teammates. In a local church, when someone offends you, all you have to do is sit on the other side of the church! But on the mission field, you can't live like that; you have to *deal* with the problem. God will allow you to be offended until you are no longer "offendable."

I also know that almost everything that happens to us concerning offenses is a direct result of the way we see or think about a situation or person. I would suggest every missionary take with him to the field a book called *Telling Yourself the Truth* by William Backus and Marie Chapian. If you're single, this book will help you bring balance to your thoughts and change what you're thinking about yourself and your teammates.

Identifying a Ministry Target Group

Our Bible school, Living Word Training Center, is the heartbeat of the ministry. In order for the Bible school to operate, there must be a team emphasis. The school is the main reason why the Keys to Freedom Ministries team exists.

In 1990, our school was a Bible school that had a target or goal to raise up leaders for the Philippines only. But that has since changed, and God used us as a team to bring about that change.

One of the great advantages of team ministry is that God will begin to speak and give new direction to the entire team in the same season. For example, in 1992, one of our Filipino staff members was the first to hear from God about the change in direction for the Bible school. He saw that God would use our school to train Filipinos to go as missionaries throughout *all of Asia*, not just within our nation.

The more we prayed about this as a team, the more sure we were this was God. The Lord began to drop this new vision inside each of us, and we began to work toward that objective.

Vision is a process. It has taken two years of teaching about going into all of Asia to get the Filipinos to believe that they, too, can "go."

We just recently sent one of our Filipino teaching staff members into Vietnam. He is a graduate of our school. God used this young man mightily while he was there. Then, during the end of 1992, God showed me that not only would we train Filipinos to "go," but that God would be sending leaders from all over Asia to prepare at the Bible school for the great harvest of this continent.

This school year we admitted our first inter-Asian student from Korea. She is called to the teaching ministry. God is truly a master strategist!

The next phase of vision development in our ministry was adding a second year to our studies. We will begin this soon; we're in the planning and preparation stages of it now. We're excited about the addition of specialization courses. For example, in the future, a student's major could be the Pastoral Ministry, and his minor could be the Teaching Ministry or Youth or Children's Ministry.

Although we just moved into our new school location, we still lack individual classroom space for seven new courses that we are instituting. So we are creating outdoor teaching environments. We just purchased new chairs, Formica boards, and easels (we had the Formica boards and aluminum easels made here in the Philippines and saved a lot of money).

Eventually, we will have more buildings, but for now, we will pour a concrete floor, add four coco lumber poles, and put a nipa thatch roof on top of the poles. The weather here is hot all year, so this will work very well for us.

If you're called to start a Bible school in a third-world nation, feeding your students will be a factor. Our school is a residence school; we house and feed 40 students. Next year, we will house 70 students. God gave us several ways to offset this cost: We have our own vegetable garden; we raise our own chickens; and we have various fruit trees.

In addition to academic studies, students at Living Word Training Center also receive daily practical-ministry training. This enables them to develop ministry skills and learn important lessons in self-discipline, team work, and interpersonal relationships.

Our practical-ministry training includes various outreaches established by the training center, such as: street witnessing, jail ministry, house-to-house evangelism, hospital ministry, follow-up, and a Bible-study program.

We set a very aggressive goal of getting 40 Christian families established in the Word through our new Bible-study program. This program has had a great impact on our area of the Philippines, and we have already reached our goal!

All 40 families were saved through our evangelistic outreach. After going through our very effective follow-up program for four weeks, they began regularly attending one of our Bible-study groups.

Our Bible-study program lasts seven months. At the end of the seven months, our goal is to leave disciple-makers in every area we have evangelized! We are very serious about winning families to the Lord.

God placed the Bible-study program in my heart as a vision He wanted me to develop. In the program, we're using the book *Getting a Grip on the Basics* by Beth Jones, who is also a RHEMA graduate. You can purchase it from the RHEMA Bible Church Bookstore in Broken Arrow, Oklahoma, among other places. I highly recommend this book.

One of the things to remember when working with a team is that every new idea takes time for acceptance. So if you present a new vision, sell it! Most people have good ideas; they just don't know how to communicate them to get others to accept and embrace them!

A vision ineffectively expressed is like a bird that can't fly: The bird has all the right equipment, but he never actually "takes off," *utilizing* his equipment.

Every week I teach the Bible-study leaders' meeting. In every meeting, I go over the vision of the program. I did that at the beginning stages of the program, and I continue to do it today. I speak out the vision, and I have the leaders repeat it. We even made a huge billboard for the classroom to help keep the vision before them.

When I first had it on my heart to develop the Bible-study program, I continually discussed the vision with the ministry staff. I also discussed it with the other missionaries. At one point, everybody on the campus was talking about the program! We all got involved. We just walked out what we saw on the inside, in our hearts. The program is only five months old, and we already have 40 strong Christian families in the program!

Training Pastors

When you first get to the mission field, you'll probably spend a lot of time developing relationships with the local pastors. Relationships are the key to being effective in the nation to which you are called. In the nation where I serve, the people are very people-oriented. They will tell you, "People are our national resource."

Get to know the men and women of God in your country. Learn what needs they have in their churches. A ministers' meeting or a pastors' meeting is an excellent use of time and a good financial investment. You can reach 50 to 100 churches at one time. If you are consistently returning to a specific area, you will see change and growth in the churches and in the men of God who lead those churches.

With a ministry team such as ours, we are individually free to develop whatever ministry outreaches God puts in our hearts. This gives us a sense of independence, yet we know we have a safety net! We are also completely responsible for the finances to fund whatever outreaches we develop. This makes us careful stewards of our partners' investment.

Conducting Ministers' Meetings

The first and foremost guideline I could suggest to you about your overseas ministry is, don't just do things to justify your existence in that country. Seek God; get *His* plan. For example, where is the group of pastors He desires you to teach? Spend much time in prayer for that group. It's important that you know not only *who* to teach but also *when* and *how*.

Other suggested guidelines for hosting ministers' meetings:

1. **When hosting a ministers' meeting such as a pastors' seminar, have a local pastor and his church be your host-church for that city.**

   Find the "influencer" of that city, the pastor that everybody listens to and respects.

2. **Pre-seminar preparation time should be at least three months.**

   There may be no phones where you minister, so unless you want a very small group of pastors at your meeting, it's best to go yourself or send one of your staff members to prepare for the meeting.

3. **Visit the location and attend whatever ministerial fellowship they have in that city.**

   Share your heart with these pastors; get them excited enough to help you put the word out about the meeting. Then expect that they won't! Go back a month before the meeting and get them excited about it again.

4. **Stress that the seminar will be non-denominational!**

   This is a great way to ensure that all the local pastors and their workers will attend.

5. **You should find the meeting place yourself or at least see it before the seminar.**

6. **See the meeting in action in your head; pay attention to all the details that need to be attended to.**

   For example, picture yourself entering the room where the meeting will be held. You'll see that you'll need a registration table. What about ink pens and so forth? Who will work at the table? What are the facilities like? Will you need to borrow chairs?

   Most churches in our part of the world do not even have 100 people in their congregations, so more than likely there won't be 100 chairs available in one church. That's another reason for finding the "influencer." He will know how to help you find the things you need.

I remember my very first pastors' seminar in Naval. I thought I had all the details worked out, but one slipped past me. The day before the seminar, after traveling alone for six hours, I arrived at the meeting place to look at the buildings.

We were going to use the buildings at the site for the meeting and for overnight lodging for 100 pastors.

It was horrible! The place was very dirty. There were dog droppings all over the floor, and the bathrooms — oh, my! I had to clean that entire place myself because I forgot a detail.

7. **Will you be using any multi-media equipment? Remember, you'll have to carry it there yourself.**

Also, don't expect to have any supplies available when you arrive at your meeting place, not even an extension cord.

8. **What about lodging? Many of these pastors will be coming from a distance.**

You could talk with the pastors of several local churches to inquire if the visiting pastors can sleep in their churches. This is a normal, common practice.

9. **What about food? The pastors may be at your seminar for several days.**

We personally feed all the pastors who attend our seminars. You might consider hiring a cook from one of the local churches.

10. **Your teaching will be more effective to more people through the years if you photocopy your lessons and distribute them.**

For my seminars, I put together a packet of the entire lesson I teach.

11. **Always plan a fun activity in addition to the teachings.**

Some of the pastors will be *past* the point of burn-out.

These are just some simple suggestions for planning your seminars. Adapt them for your own use, as every country and place where you minister will be different.

Itinerating Overseas

Can a single female missionary be effective itinerating, traveling alone throughout the nation to which she is called? Yes! As I said, there's grace for whatever the Lord has called you to do.

Any woman God has called to the mission field, single or married, has special grace from God to accomplish the task. My favorite scripture is Luke 1:45 in the *Amplified* translation: ". . . blessed — happy, to be envied — is she who believed that there would be a fulfillment of the things that were spoken to her from the Lord."

During my first year in the Philippines, I preached and taught the Word of God more than 280 times. That included teaching in our school plus traveling every weekend by bus, boat, or jeepney.

I have had so many wonderful adventures traveling and bringing the Word of God to people. Once people find out you're willing to come and teach them the Word, they will keep you busy! My schedule is booked eight to ten months in advance.

I fell in love with the Filipino people by visiting them where they live. I have slept on hundreds of wooden floors and on tops of tables because the floors were dirt floors. I've climbed mountains, ridden in pump boats (small canoe-type boats) in 12-foot waves, and walked through human refuse to board boats where there were no docks. I think back on some of those experiences and smile. *It is worth it!*

When you finally arrive at your ministry destination and people are gathered in crowds at the church, eagerly waiting for a message from God, you realize it's worth everything it took to get you there!

I've seen God touch people and move on them in such beautiful ways. By living here and learning about the people, I've learned how to minister to their needs. God desires to minister to His people, and there is a great move of God in the Philippines! Our part in the local churches is to teach people and help create an expectancy and a desire for the things of God. God moves where the people *desire* Him to move. Desire *for* God comes from knowledge *about* God.

How We Began Ministering to Hurting Children

Another ministry venture the Lord placed in my heart is called "Jesus Loves Street Children," a ministry outreach to abused and homeless children.

In 1992, I spent a season in prayer asking God to really show me the Filipino people. I wanted to see their spiritual needs. I wanted to see the ugliness that Satan had brought about in their lives to oppress and rob them. There were many ways in which I had refused to see it.

One Sunday morning as I was preparing to go to a city to share the Word, I was sitting on a bus in downtown Catbalogan. As I looked out the window, I saw a sight too horrible for my American eyes.

There were two children lying on the sidewalk, asleep in the dirt. I quickly turned my head away. God said, "No, you prayed to see; now *look*." I looked and I thought of Matthew 9:36: "*. . .when he [Jesus] saw the multitudes, he was moved with compassion on them, because they fainted, and were scattered abroad, as sheep having no shepherd.*"

These were scattered and confused children. They were homeless and had no one. It was a long time before I did anything about what I saw. God had to really work with me. I wasn't a children's teacher; I teach adults. But God gave me the ability to organize a program for them to get His work accomplished.

The first thing I had to do was go to the government social workers to find out how many street children there were in that city. They didn't know. They were excited about what God told me to do and began to help me find them.

We were able to gather 30 children. We began helping them with basic things. I hired a cook, and one Filipino children's worker and another missionary agreed to help teach the children. We began bathing the children, feeding them, and teaching them the Word of God.

God did not tell me to start a home at that time. He just told me to bathe and feed them and teach them the Word — and especially that Jesus loves them.

We have seen incredible progress with these children in the last two years. I also know that some of these children will one day attend our Bible school, as some of them are leaders with a call of God on their lives.

For a location for Jesus Loves Street Children, we began by using a room in a government building. Then the number of children began to grow — 30, 40, 52 — and this was in the first year! But the Lord and my ministry partners, my supporters, were faithful.

Just recently, I received the go-ahead from God to start a home for the children. It took time finding a place that would accommodate our needs, but I finally found the perfect place. It needs a lot of work, but I was able to get a five-year lease and a small building next to it to use as a classroom. There's land for a vegetable garden, and we'll also raise chickens. The name of the home will be "God's Town."

A Last Word to Those Who Know They're To 'Go' — Especially to Singles

Whether you're single or married, I encourage you to do some studying and get to know your role models — those who have gone to the field before you.

To those of you who are single and female like me, get to know your sisters of the past. For example, missionary Johanna Veenstra, who served God in Africa at the turn of the century, said in essence about her work: "There has been no sacrifice on my part because the Lord Jesus Himself was my constant companion."

You can also read about Mary Slessor of Calabar. I have read her life story three times since I've been here in the Philippines. Sustained by her faith in God and a sense of His divine Presence, she planted churches, schools, and even started a hospital.

I've told the Lord many times, "If you can use me in any way, here I am." And if God can use Johanna Veenstra, Mary Slessor — and *me* — He can use you, too, and He *wants* too!

The only thing we have to offer Him are these lives we're living. So let's offer Him all of our days, and in obedience to His will and timing, be faithful to "*go*."

Chapter 9

Single — and Female — on the Foreign Field

By Melinda (Osburn) Koehler ('84 '85)

Melinda Koehler graduated from Portland State University in 1982 with a degree in Health Education. She graduated from RHEMA Bible Training Center in May 1985 and from Victory World Missions Training Center in December 1985. She moved to Zaire, Central Africa, as a missionary in January 1986.

Melinda's husband, Dan, graduated from Central Michigan University in 1985 with a degree in physics, mathematics, and computer science. He worked at Dow chemical corporation before attending RHEMA in 1986 and graduating in 1987.

Dan went to Zaire, where he met Melinda, in December 1988 (Melinda interpreted for Dan during his first year on the field). Dan and Melinda married in January 1991. They have two children: Hannah, born Stateside in September 1992, and Caleb, born in Nairobi, Kenya, in June 1994.

The Koehlers have worked in Zaire for a combined total of nine years, preaching faith seminars, teaching in Bible schools, and translating the Hagins' books into the Swahili and Kinyarwanda languages. They have recently begun a new work in Rwanda, a country where no faith-teaching churches have existed. The Koehlers are starting a church, a Bible school, and elementary schools.

From the time I was seven years old, I knew I was called to be a missionary! At seven, I was involved in a serious accident and was hospitalized for about a week. One night during my hospital stay, my mother dreamed that I had died. She woke up frightened and immediately called the hospital.

The hospital staff assured my mother that I was fine and told her to go back to sleep. When she fell asleep again, she was awakened by the same dream. She called the hospital a second time, and they continued to reassure my mother of my well-being.

When my mother had the same dream the third time, she could not go back to sleep. Instead, she fell to her knees, pleading with God to spare my life. She told the Lord that "if He would let me live," she would dedicate all the days of my life to Him.

Suddenly, my mother saw a vision. In the vision, she saw me at about forty years of age with my husband. We had a very determined look on our faces to serve God no matter what came. My mother then sensed in her spirit that I would live many miles away from her, but she knew God was confirming to her that I would live and not die.

My mother didn't tell me about that vision until many years later. But immediately after I was released from the hospital, I began telling everyone that I was going to be a missionary to Africa! I didn't know what a missionary was or even where *Africa* was, but God had taken my mother's prayer to heart and placed a missions call in my spirit!

Follow God's Plan Step by Step

After high school, God directed me to go to college before attending RHEMA Bible Training Center and to earn a degree in Health Education. In retrospect, I can see why He led me to obtain a college degree. Having a degree earns me respect from foreign governments. Foreign governments are more interested in projects you can accomplish for them than they are in evangelism or Bible teaching. Presently, we are starting Christian elementary schools in Rwanda.

I attended RHEMA from 1983 to 1985. God used the people I met during that time to support the ministry and to give me "divine connections" to the field in which He wanted me — *Africa.*

During the two years I was at RHEMA, I meditated on scriptures about being led by the Holy Spirit, and I prayed about where God would lead me. (Don't wait until you finish Bible school to begin praying about where to go!) I constantly kept my heart sensitive and open to God so I would be listening and hearing clearly when He directed me.

During my second year at RHEMA while listening to one of our missionary-teachers, Ralph Hagemeier, during a missions class, I heard a Voice behind me say, "You will work with him." I thought one of the other students was playing a trick on me! I looked behind me to see who it was, but everyone was listening intently to Rev. Hagemeier.

Then I heard the Voice again: "One day you will work with that man." So I said on the inside of me, *Well, Lord, if this is You talking to me, You will have to open the door.* God was true to His Word and nine months later I was with the Hagemeiers in Kalemie, Zaire.

Wait Before God and Let *Him* Open Your Door of Opportunity!

Once you've heard from God about His will for your life, you can just sit back and let God open the door for you. You don't have to force your ministry on anyone. God will open the door before you in the place where He wants you.

I believe that the most important thing that has helped me receive direction from God is praying in the Holy Spirit. Every time I face a decision in life, I increase my time of praying in tongues because it makes me more receptive and sensitive to the leading of the Lord.

As I've prayed in the Spirit and taken time to wait on the Lord first, I've never had a doubt about any decision I've ever made. I also stand in faith on such scriptures as John 10:3-5, First Corinthians 2:16, Proverbs 3:5 and 6, and Romans 8:14 and 16. For example, I'll confess what John 10:4 and 5 says: "I know the Voice of my Shepherd, and the voice of a stranger I shall not follow." God is so faithful to guide us!

The Importance of Being Spirit-Led in *Every* Area of Life

I can't stress enough how important it is to pray, to stand on the Word, and to be led by the Holy Spirit. Just recently, my husband, Dan, and I had an inward warning about a trip we were going to take, but we didn't take the time to stop and pray to find out what God was warning us about. (Dan and I married in 1991 and have been serving God in Africa ever since.)

We were going to Kigali, Rwanda, to minister over the Easter holiday. I was pregnant at the time. From Kigali we were going to take a plane to Nairobi, Kenya, so I could get a prenatal checkup.

We had wanted to fly from our hometown to Kigali and then on to Nairobi but decided to drive to Kigali and fly to Nairobi from there, saving ourselves $100. Well, the day after we flew out of Kigali to Nairobi was the day the president of Rwanda was assassinated. Our vehicle that we left parked in Kigali was stolen in all the pillaging that took place.

If we had taken the time to find out what God was warning us about, we would have flown to Kigali instead of driving. If we had taken the time to pray, we wouldn't have been so concerned about saving $100 on a flight while losing a $27,000 Land Cruiser in the meantime!

So be sure to take the time to listen to God and be sensitive to His leading. It could be a matter of life or death.

The Value of Experience and Preparation

When I graduated from RHEMA in 1985, I was filled with God's Word but had never had any experience on a foreign field. (Until then, just going from Oregon to Oklahoma was as foreign as I had gotten!) I felt like I needed some hands-on experience, so I took two short-term trips.

My first trip was to Mexico City, Mexico, shortly after the devastating earthquake of October 1985. There we saw 500 people born again in a week. My second trip was to Quezaltenango, Guatemala, where we saw 700 people born again in four days! Those trips helped give me experience in working on a foreign field and in using an interpreter.

I believe taking short-term trips is one of the most valuable experiences anyone can have who feels called to missions. It will take away much of the "fear of the unknown" and give you confidence as to how God can use you.

Make Faith Your Way of Life!

Finances are always a major obstacle in mission work. God directs some people to itinerate to raise support, and that is especially important if you have a family. But as a single lady going on the field, I didn't have the needs that a family has — money for children's food, clothing, schooling, and so forth. God directed me to make plans to go to Africa, assuring me that He would meet my needs.

Not raising support goes against what is generally taught in missions, but the key to success in any ministry is to learn to follow the inward witness of the Holy Spirit and to be obedient to what God directs *you* to do! He told me to "just go," so I did!

My mind told me I was crazy. Well-meaning folks who were very close to me sat me down to explain how I couldn't survive on the mission field. Who would take care of me?

But I had gotten well-acquainted with my Heavenly Father while at school, and I knew that since He had gotten me through school, He would continue to be faithful to me even on the mission field.

Traveling to the other side of the world alone made me even more aware of God's Presence. There is something special about a situation in which it's just you and God. It provides a marvelous opportunity for God to show Himself big on your behalf.

Once I had to travel from Zaire to Dar es Salaam, Tanzania, to get a car out of port. I spent a month traveling alone across half the continent. When it came time to cross Lake Tanganyika, I boarded a passenger ship. The car was to follow on a barge later.

On the ship, some young men spied me all alone — the only white lady traveling on the ship. They started to harass me, saying some rather wicked things.

I could have had a pity-party, saying, "Poor me, traveling all alone." Or I could make the most of the opportunity. So I decided that if those men were going to be bold for the devil, I was going to be *more* bold for my *God*!

I began witnessing to those young men, and I told them if they were saved they wouldn't talk like that. I then explained how to be born again and to become a new creature.

Before I knew it, there was a crowd of about 40 people gathered who wanted to hear what "this white lady" had to say! So I grabbed my Swahili Bible and preached to a captive audience for about two hours! Then I gave an altar call. Eighteen people accepted the Lord, and fourteen were immediately filled with the Spirit and spoke with tongues — right there on the top deck of the ship!

We can turn every situation around for the glory of God — even traveling alone across Africa!

The Just Shall Live By Faith
Even in the Area of Finances — Even on the Mission Field

As soon as I finished Bible school, I made preparations to go to the mission field even though I had only $10 a month in pledged support and no money in-hand. Two days before I left I was given $1,000. I took my checkbook and was able to write a check every month to cover my needs. (In Africa, there is usually someone in every town who is anxious to get an American-dollar check and who will be able to give you local currency.)

Every month afterward, God would touch the hearts of different people, and the money came in — more than enough for my needs (which at that time was only $500-$1000 a month). There was even enough for my ticket to fly back home to the States after two years! Most of my support was from sources I never would have guessed. God likes to use the least-suspected avenue!

Dan's testimony as a single man on the field is almost the same as mine. He left without ever itinerating with only $45 a month pledged to him for support. On the mission field, however, he usually received about $500 a month.

God has been just as faithful to us even after we were married. One year we had many extra expenses because of having our first baby, and it looked like we might go under financially. While we were at Kenneth Hagin Ministries' Campmeeting that year in Tulsa, Oklahoma, Dan felt led to sow $1,000 into RHEMA Bible Training Center. My mind was racing. I thought, *Yeah, but where in the world are we going to get that kind of money?* But I set myself in agreement with Dan, and we decided to send in $200 every month for five months.

The very month we finished paying our pledge, someone who wasn't even on our mailing list found someone who knew our address so he could send us $10,000!

Have a God-Given Purpose in Ministry

While I was at RHEMA, God revealed to me my part in His ministry. He gave me a threefold vision or plan:

1. To be an extension of Rev. Kenneth E. Hagin in teaching faith to Africa via Bible seminars. This plan would include spending several weeks at a time in one area of the bush if necessary.

2. To raise up Bible training centers where nationals could be taught to reach their own people with the Gospel.

    This plan creates a multiplication effect. For example, in Zaire there are more than 200 different dialects, and it is impossible to learn all of their languages. But we can teach nationals to reach their own people with the word of faith.

3. To translate Rev. Hagin's books and other faith books into the languages of the people.

    There may not always be an open door for hands-on ministry in these countries, but the written Word can go into and *remain* in places that we can't. So far, we have translated many books into the Swahili and Kinyarwanda languages.

Don't Compromise Your Call

God had given me a very specific vision to fulfill, and I knew that if I were to marry, I would have to marry a man with exactly the same calling. There had been many nice men who were interested in me, but I could not compromise the call of God on my life. It is better to be single till the rapture and fulfill God's purpose than to marry the wrong person and miss God's divine plan. But if you are obedient to "*go*," God can bring your mate to you even on the mission field like He did for me!

I knew Dan was the one for me because he had exactly the same vision from God that I had. Before I met Dan, I had never shared extensively with anyone on earth the vision God had put in my heart. Yet one evening as Dan and I were just sharing about the work of God, Dan explained his vision for Africa, and it was word for word the plan God had secretly placed in *my* heart for Africa! I then knew he was the one for me, and for the last four years since we married, we have been working together, fulfilling that vision.

Recently we moved from Zaire to Kigali, Rwanda, and we are pioneering a new work there. We started a church by getting a music group together to sing God's praises in a country that has a spirit of murder and gloom over it.

As we sing, people come to listen, and we are able to give them the Good News. Soon we will start a Bible school as well as elementary schools. (Most of the teachers were slaughtered in the genocide, and now the education system must start all over again.)

Advantages of Single Missionary Life

I am grateful that I came to the field as a single, because in many ways it made me a more effective missionary. Paul said in First Corinthians 7:34 and 35 that the unmarried woman is devoted to God in both body and spirit. How true it is! As an unmarried lady I was able to give myself in undivided devotion to the Lord and to His work. I was able to learn the language much faster than many of my married coworkers because I had more time to myself — more time to spend in prayer and study.

Learning the language is essential if you plan to work in an area for an extended period of time. The single women in our particular mission have always been the most successful in learning the language because of being able to give undivided attention to studying. But maybe the reason they learn the language faster is that ladies like to talk a little more and are more willing to learn the language by making some mistakes!

The Pitfalls

Housing is perhaps the most difficult aspect of going out on the field as a single lady. Unless you go with a previously chosen roommate, you might have to room with whomever is already there. Women frequently have trouble finding a compatible roommate. The pressures are high enough living in a third-world country and standing out "like a sore thumb" as a person of a different race. It would be difficult having to deal with strife in your home setting as well.

So make the selection of a roommate a top priority in prayer. Women in general tend to be more finicky about how they like their houses kept. It is better to live alone or try to go to the field with someone you already know is compatible with you. This can alleviate many problems.

Someone once said, "I'd love missions if it weren't for the other missionaries." Unfortunately, that can be too true sometimes. If you get in a difficult situation, remember, the key to victory is love and forgiveness. When you live by those rules, you will eventually win every time.

I had a situation when I first went on the field in which both of my roommates chose not to like me before they even met me! My roommates' hurtful words devastated me at first. But I was determined to continue walking in love and kindness regardless of how they treated me. It wasn't easy, and it took over a year to really win them. But I'm glad to say that because I continued to walk in love, the very ones who hurt me the most are some of my closest friends now.

Another thing that is especially difficult for single women is working in the ministry with men. In developing countries, most women are not educated. In fact, in Zaire, very few women can even read and write. When I first went to Zaire, I found that the women there would not accept me because I was not married and didn't have any children. We had nothing in common. Try as I would to reach out to them, most women looked down on me in the African culture. But since I've married and have had children, I have had some tremendous women's meetings.

When I was single, most of my ministry was directed to the Bible school students and to the church body as a whole. The students especially were very enthusiastic about learning the Word. Several of them even said that the reason God sent them to the Bible school was to get the teaching on faith and on Mark 11:23 and 24 that I gave them. It was revolutionary to their lives.

Single life is especially difficult in the African culture because adultery is a rampant problem even in the Church. When people are living in sin, they expect that everyone else is like them. The important thing to do is to avoid even the "appearance of evil."

It is difficult to know at first just what people may be thinking in another culture, but try to be sensitive. As in any ministry, avoid being alone with anyone of the opposite sex or spending any extended time with him or her. Then you won't provide opportunity for people to talk. God will always vindicate you as you seek to keep your way pure.

Dealing With Loneliness

Those long African nights! Darkness comes to Africa at 6:00 p.m. and stays until 6:00 a.m. So there are twelve hours of dark and twelve hours of light. As a single on the field, there is potential for loneliness. There is nothing to do in the bush of Africa after dark. I realize other cultures are not so backward, but there were many long nights when I was alone. It is hard when others are home with their families and you are alone. Bringing good reading materials or having a television and VCR can be a tremendous blessing (that is, *if* you have electricity).

God Will Give You Grace for the Task
And Rewards for Your Obedience!

A benefit of being single is having more opportunity to bond with the nationals. Before I was married I spent most of my time with the nationals or ministering. I was booked up for ministry every week for three months in advance and could have accepted more invitations if I had wanted to. I was able to pour myself 100 percent into the study and ministry of God's Word. Although living alone is a great challenge, what makes it worth the sacrifice is seeing people being set free by God's Word.

When I would go through a difficult time and begin to think that the sacrifice was too great, God would give me an extra measure of His anointing and grace, and ministry would be even sweeter.

After a particularly difficult time, I remember one lady who had been a spiritualist who got saved in one of my meetings. I was teaching about the Father God and sharing my testimony of God's care for me. This lady's husband had left her with five children, and she made her living by talking to the spirits of the dead. When she heard how God had cared for me thousands of miles away from home, she knew that He could care for her too. She repented for serving the devil and was gloriously saved. As I remained faithful during those hard times, God would reward with extraordinary blessings.

There is prejudice against singles on the mission field that I never experienced in the States. Seemingly, everyone is suspicious. A friend of mine working with a particular organization had a discouraging time and eventually returned home. She wanted to work in partnership with another family among the pygmies, but her leadership was afraid of an adulterous situation developing just because she was single without a partner. She said, "I feel like I'm guilty until proven innocent." Her superior said, "You are!"

There is a lot working against the single woman, but you can win and prove that you can live to the glory of God above sin and reproach.

Pay the Price To Keep
Yourself Spiritually Strong

It is a great challenge to keep yourself built up spiritually. There is usually no one else to feed you. In every place we have worked, there was never anyone else who believed the way we do. There is *rarely* another Spirit-filled person around, but almost *never* is there a word-of-faith person.

I found it important to bring along faith-building books and tapes. I like reading books by Smith Wigglesworth, John Lake, and Lilian B. Yeomans. After my first term in Africa, I found that bringing my books from Bible school were far more important than just about anything else — even more important than my blow dryer and curling iron!

Building my faith daily in the areas of healing and protection is essential. We are in an area where there are no doctors, telephones, or any type of help from the outside. This is a great opportunity to put into practice what we learned at RHEMA!

Be an Example to Other Missionaries

Fellowship with others of like-precious faith is important. I so value that fellowship. Unfortunately, there are no "faith" people in our part of the country. In Bukavu, Zaire, we had an English fellowship on Sunday nights, but it bothered me to hear so much unbelief at times. When I was going through a trial, I had to avoid going to the fellowship so I wouldn't face opposition to what I was believing God for. But we can fellowship with other missions around the Savior. Some of my best friends on the field have been from other missions such as Anglican and Conservative Baptist.

It is important to be a good witness to other missionaries too. My Baptist friend said that she was able to learn so much from me that she had to reevaluate her own doctrine. Another Pentecostal missionary with whom I came in contact in Kinshasa (Zaire's capital city) told me something negative about every faith person she had ever known and said that they were all "flakes"!

For example, several of them had been foolish and had gone bankrupt while confessing that their taxes had been paid. At that time, I was seeking an exoneration from the government for the Land Cruiser that had been donated to me. Exonerations were not often given, but I knew God had one for me!

This Pentecostal missionary kept telling me how impossible it was and that I would never get the exoneration. She said that even well-established missions had failed to receive one, so our mission that hadn't even received all of its government papers would never be able to get an exoneration.

Every time this missionary gave me a bad report, I went back to my prayer closet and told God what she said. Then I reminded God what I believed about Him. He is bigger than any government office! He is bigger than all the corruption of the Zaire government! He is bigger than bad reports!

A couple of days later when this missionary came to visit, without saying a word to her, I just showed her my exoneration papers. She started to cry and said, "Melinda, you are the first person I have ever seen faith work for!" Praise God that we can be an example not only to the nationals, but also to the other missionaries!

Newsletters Are a *Must*

Something that I feel to be very important is monthly newsletters. Newsletters keep your partners informed as to what area of ministry you are currently involved in and help your partners stay hooked up with you. In your newsletters, it is especially important to share day-to-day stories with them about what life is like on the mission field.

It is not so important to preach to them in the letters, but to let them feel like they are a part of your life. Let your life be a testimony of what you preach! People in the States get preached at enough. What they really want to know is: What kind of bugs or snakes do you have to deal with? What kind of food do you eat? What are your accommodations like?

So share everyday happenings, using words like "The other day a strange thing happened..."

Life in a foreign land is so different from life as we are used to it. So share the differences in cultures with your partners. My partners say they can hardly wait for our letters every month because they should be entitled "Adventures with Dan and Melinda"!

For example, just recently, I experienced the trial of my missionary life — eating the dreaded dagaa! A favorite food in Zaire is these little fish called dagaa that are like minnows (used as a fishing bait in the States). For almost two years, I had successfully managed to avoid eating them. But one day I walked into the Bible school's cafeteria when the students were eating dagaa, and they invited me to eat with them.

I could see the disappointment on their faces as I made a dozen excuses why I couldn't. So I accepted the invitation and sat down to a plate of these ugly fish with their little beady eyes staring at me! I breathed deeply and downed the first one. The sand in the fish made a crunching sound between my teeth. I almost choked! I did manage to eat two of them before excusing myself. The students were so thrilled that I had eaten with them that I soon became their favorite teacher.

These everyday sort of incidents (and believe me, they are everyday!) are fun things to share with your partners.

Also remember, don't look to the churches or your newsletter as your source for support. God is always our source, but we do have a responsibility to keep informed those who are praying for and supporting us.

Don't Fall Into the Bitterness Trap

A frequent trap I see missionaries fall into is bitterness. It is hard to be away from the States and family and friends. The devil would try to discourage you and make you think that no one thinks of you or cares. I have gone many times for long periods of time with no letters. I felt hurt and forgotten by everyone. I would think, *Here I am struggling on the backside of the desert trying to get the Word into a bunch of stiff-necked people, and nobody cares!*

It's easy to get jealous or bitter or to have a pity-party. But it's during those times that you have an opportunity to praise God and not lose your joy. If we are faithful to fulfill the ministry that God has given us, there will be rewards.

Someday when we are at the Marriage Supper of the Lamb (you can look for me seated in the Zairian section eating heavenly ugali and dagaa!), there will be those who will say, "Thank you, Melinda, for coming to us with the Word. We are here only because you came!" The temporal sacrifices we make are nothing compared to the eternal rewards that are being stored up for us.

Nobody owes us anything. Some missionaries have tried to make the folks back home feel guilty for not doing more. We don't try to extract money from anyone or to heap guilt upon them. Even in the States, our goal is to minister to the pastor and the people of the churches we visit. As we minister to the church's needs, God always sees to it that our needs are met too. If you really believe that God alone is your source, then all the striving to raise support will just fall by the wayside.

Raising support is a great opportunity to use your faith and begin confessing that God is raising up people to hook up with your vision. Claim favor scriptures in prayer over churches and pastors. If we do our homework in prayer, then God can open the doors He has for us.

What You Preach Must Be Real to You

During my first term, I really needed a vehicle. It was a temptation to want to look to various churches or individuals to meet that need. But God reminded me that He alone was my source. Many times I had to walk or use public transportation, or I had to borrow a vehicle from other missionaries.

I remember one Sunday I walked to three different services and had blisters all over my feet. I saw it as a faith challenge, so as I walked, I thanked God for my new car and claimed more souls for the Kingdom of God. I wanted to be an example to the Zairian people in word and in deed. I wanted to show them how to trust God for their needs as I was trusting Him for mine.

God was faithful, and sometime later Kenneth Copeland Ministries donated a brand-new Toyota Land Cruiser to me. Everywhere I had preached on faith, I'd told the people that God was going to give me a car. They went wild with excitement and rejoiced when they saw that beautiful truck I named "Nsango Malamu" (meaning the Good News in the Lingala language). Our ministry is worthless if we can't live what we preach.

Love Never Fails

My motto in ministry is a quote from Lloyd John Ogilvie. He said, "When people know how much you care, then they will care how much you know!" I've seen missionaries become militant and hard on people, like an army major would. This isolated these missionaries from the nationals, and it made the missionaries bitter about their rejection. They wondered why the people wouldn't accept them! But what draws people is compassion and love. Your ministry will never amount to anything if you don't show the love of God. Love never fails!

Chapter 10

Remaining Faithful to Your Vision

By Bill ('89 '90) and Shelli Pafford ('89 '90)

Five months after Bill and Shelli Pafford graduated from RHEMA Bible Training Center, they were on the mission field in the Philippines. Since that time, the Paffords have been working with missionaries Paul and Shoddy Chase, teaching and training nationals for ministry at Living Word Training Center. Bill and Shelli also conduct church meetings throughout the Philippines.

The Paffords know that they will be moving to China one day soon as missionaries to that nation, doing the same kind of work they are currently doing. They have three children: Scott, age 11; Brad, age 10; and Brittany, age 6.

Years before we ever attended RHEMA Bible Training Center, we knew we would be missionaries to China one day. Although we haven't yet reached China as of this writing, the time is drawing closer. Even so, everything we are doing now on the mission field in the Philippines is preparing us for the things we will be doing in China.

One thing I've learned — preparation time is not wasted time, but it gets you ready for what is ahead. The beauty of it is that even now, we are changing the lives and the eternal destinies of people in Asia.

The Lord spoke to me about China one afternoon while I was worshipping Him in my living room at home. He said, "I'm raising up people in China who will become for Me evangelists, pastors, and teachers. And you'll be a part of those whom I'll send there to teach and train them."

Well, as I said, we haven't reached China yet, but even now, *God is preparing us to minister there.* China is always in our hearts. We can't go to Africa — Africa is not in our hearts. We can pray for Africa. We could *visit* Africa. But we couldn't live there; it's just not in our hearts.

Africa is not a part of God's plan for my life. Our Father God has other people prepared for Africa. But China keeps rising up out of my heart. I'm going there! I'm going to live there and be there as a missionary sent by God to that nation. I'm going there to share the Good News and to heal the sick through faith in Jesus Christ!

The Lord said something interesting to Paul when He appeared to him on the road to Damascus:

ACTS 26:16,18

16 But rise, and stand upon thy feet: for I have appeared unto thee for this purpose, to make thee a minister and a witness both of these things which thou hast seen, and of those things in the which I will appear unto thee. . . .

18 To open their eyes, and to turn them from darkness to light, and from the power of Satan unto God, that they may receive forgiveness of sins, and inheritance among them which are sanctified by faith that is in me.

I always find myself being drawn to those scriptures; they mean something to me personally.

There are two more scriptures that just seem to be infused in my heart:

2 TIMOTHY 2:2

2 And the things that thou hast heard of me among many witnesses, the same commit thou to faithful men, who shall be able to teach others also.

PHILIPPIANS 2:13

13 For it is God which worketh in you both to will and to do of his good pleasure.

These scriptures speak to me from within my spirit and give me direction for my life. They show me what to do. To me, they are like ripples in a pond before my face, showing me God's purpose and plan for my life on the earth.

In the Philippines since October 1990, we've been preaching and teaching the things we've learned and seen about the Kingdom of God. We've been teaching and training Filipinos who are called into the ministry so they can take the Good News of Jesus Christ throughout their nation, to the other nations of Asia, and even to the other parts of the world!

We've brought revival to church congregations as we've gone to them and have taught them for one to three days at a time. Through the preaching and teaching of the Word, we've also enriched the ministries of pastors and Bible teachers, and we've taught them a fuller and more in-depth knowledge of the Scriptures.

We've ministered to them all in the grace of our Lord and with the power of the Holy Spirit. We've brought joy where there was no joy, peace where there was no peace, understanding of the will of God where there was no understanding, and knowledge of the ways and the leading of the Holy Spirit where there was no knowledge of Him. We've taught what we've learned. We've taught what works for us according to the Scriptures. We are duplicating ourselves in others in this nation — we're making disciples!

We're developing good Bible teachers who can minister to the people here and follow the leading of the Holy Spirit. We've seen *great increase* in the Body of Christ in the Philippines.

This is what God has called Shelli and me to do, and we are so glad to do it. It is a pleasure to serve the Lord in Asia!

Many, not a few, of the people we've taught know God is calling them to the nations of Asia. As God has been preparing us for China, we've been preparing others to go also — to China as well as to other Asian countries. What a joy and a privilege it is to do that!

So, again, preparation time is not wasted time. Preparation time only prepares you for those things that are ahead. When Shelli and I do get to China, we will already have many years of experience that will help us as we begin to teach and train the people of China.

Getting to the Mission Field

As I mentioned before, preparation time is not wasted time. Rather, it paves the way for God's will to be accomplished in your life.

Attending RHEMA Bible Training Center as part of our preparation not only taught us what the Scripture says, but it gave us certain wisdom about the Church and the Christian life. It also put us in the position to begin our missionary work in Asia.

After the ceremony on RHEMA's graduation night, we attended a graduation party at the Ninowski Recreation Center. I overheard two of my friends talking about future ministry, and I said to them, "Don't worry about what you'll be doing in the future; just enjoy this graduation night. The Lord will show you later what He wants you to do."

Shelli and I were not anxious about the future, for we already knew that somehow, and at some time, we were going to the mission field and to China.

For years before attending RHEMA and while attending RHEMA, we knew that we'd be going to China one day. During the last few months we were at RHEMA, I knew that within a year we would be on the mission field. I didn't know how it would all work out, but I assumed we would be in China within one year.

In five months, well within the one year, we *were* on the mission field — not in China — but in the Philippines. God has been using us in the Philippines and preparing us for what is ahead at the same time.

The day after graduation from RHEMA, a fellow classmate and good friend came to us and invited us to hear a missionary from Asia who would be in town that day. Shelli and I quickly decided to go. We were just glad to go and hear a seasoned missionary speak. We had no expectations of actually joining up with him or his ministry.

Well, to shorten the story, during missionary Paul Chase's time of sharing that day, it came into both of our hearts *to begin our missionary work in the Philippines, working with Paul Chase and his wife, Shoddy*!

The next week we returned from RHEMA to our home church in Lakeland, Florida, Family Worship Center, which is pastored by Reggie Scarborough. We shared with him how we came to our decision to go to the Philippines, and he agreed with us. Five months later, he and the church sent us to the Philippines — to Asia — to the other side of the earth!

During the five months between our graduation from RHEMA and our first trip to the mission field, we got involved in working in our church. I began to minister again every Wednesday in the county jail. It was an established outreach of our church.

Pastor Reggie asked me to come on staff to get more ministry experience and to see more about how the church functioned. I'll always be grateful to him for his trust in me and for allowing me the opportunity to learn from his wonderful ministry. He truly is a good man who has faith in a great God, and believes for and trusts in the leadership of the Holy Spirit.

Pastor Reggie has made rich deposits in our lives, just like RHEMA has, and just like the Hagins and other great ministers of God have. Those rich deposits are for us, our family, and for the people God sends us to.

We met with Paul Chase a couple times during those five months after graduation from RHEMA. I had written down more than 100 questions for him to answer for us — and some of those questions had two or three parts! I had a lot of questions because we had never done what we were about to do. The questions were not to determine whether or not we should go, but *how* to make our first experience on the mission field more comfortable and successful. We really did not know what to expect on the mission field.

I suppose those questions did help some, but I've got to tell you, the first trip to the mission field can be a real shocker. As I said, we really didn't know what to expect. Living in modern America does not prepare you for the mission field. The poverty, the hopelessness, the habits, the ways of thinking, the lack of anything convenient, and the smells on our mission field all took some getting used to.

But we got used to it, and so can you, because of the grace that is available to those God calls. We knew God wanted us here, and we purposed in our hearts that we would follow His will.

Spiritual Preparation

Knowing the "what," "where," "when," "who," and "how" of God's will for any missionary venture is extremely important. Recovering from mistakes costs valuable time and money. It's true that some people will still be blessed through your ministry to them, but if you are not where God's wants you to be, doing what He wants you to do, then you are in the wrong place, doing the wrong thing. In other words, you aren't doing His will concerning your calling.

The missionary needs to get and *follow* God's vision for his missionary work. He will be accountable to God for that. God gives plans, purposes, and sight or vision to His missionaries. The missionary only needs to get it, receive it, and do it.

Getting those plans, purposes, and sight or vision from God isn't hard if you are doing what it takes to get them. And what it takes to get them is the same thing it takes to know the "what, where, when, who, and how" of accomplishing God's will. In other words, *maintaining close intimate fellowship with God puts you in a position to hear God's instructions.*

Prayer is so necessary in order to find out all you need to know concerning the will of God. Without communication between you and God, you can't know the will of God. If you don't know the will of God concerning your missions work, then you can't do His will in missions. It is as simple as that. Prayer is communication between you and God; it's the vehicle that puts you and your Father in contact with each other.

Prayer puts you in a position to be truly one with God in His plans and purposes for your life. It allows you the opportunity to be in agreement with God in anything and everything about your missionary work. It is through prayer that the missionary will find out the "what, where, when, who, and how" of accomplishing his missionary calling!

Without prayer — without communication between you and God — you may have an inward unction for missions, but you won't know any of the above-mentioned specifics, which you must know. So communicate with God, and He will let you know everything you need to know.

If you know you are called to be a missionary, go to a good Bible training center, like RHEMA, to learn God's Word, to get wisdom, and to learn how to practically apply God's Word to every situation of your life and ministry. Knowing God, knowing the ways of His Spirit, knowing how to be practical, and applying what you know to your life and ministry will make you a success. Isn't that what Joshua 1:8 tells us?

8 This book of the law shall not depart out of thy mouth; but thou shalt meditate therein day and night, that thou mayest observe to do according to all that is written therein: for then thou shalt make thy way prosperous, and then thou shalt have good success.

Find Something To Put Your Hand To

Even if you don't yet know all the necessary things you'll need to know to follow God's will for your missionary work, you can still get involved in the area of your calling and gain some valuable experience.

Always be moving toward what God has called you to do, even if you can't specifically do it yet. For example, hook up with another missionary and work there for a year or more. You'll learn a lot. Time on the mission field gives you an opportunity to deal with your feelings and to change in areas in which you need to change.

Getting involved will cause you to know more than you know already. Use that time as a means of "apprenticeship" until it is time for you to move into God's specific will for *you*. Getting involved will also give you direction for prayer — there are things, situations, circumstances, and daily concerns on the mission field that you could pray about ahead of time.

Plus — as an added bonus to you — even while you are helping someone else on the mission field, God can use you there. With all that valuable experience and knowledge, you will be in a better position to do what God wants you to do.

Who then should you work with? It should be someone who is proven on the mission field. If you are a RHEMA graduate, you could contact RHEMA. They can tell you of some great missionary works to hook up with that will help you develop as a missionary. As you begin to talk about certain missionary works, your spirit will have the peace of God concerning one of them. That ministry will keep coming back to your remembrance. Follow after peace. Take a step of faith (you won't die!).

Three things I always rely on are the following:

1. **The peace of God inside.**

   The peace of God is to rule in our hearts (Col. 3:15). The peace of God will surpass our understanding (Phil. 4:7). We are to pursue the things which make for peace (1 Peter 3:11).

2. **The awareness that God is working in me.**

   Philippians 2:13 says, *"For it is God which worketh in you both to will and to do of his good pleasure."* I know that God is energizing and creating in me all that is needed, not only to *know* His will, but the desire or the "want to" to *do* His will. Then He works in me the ability to help me do it!

   Psalm 37:4 and 5 says, *"Delight thyself also in the Lord; and he shall give thee the desires of thine heart. Commit thy way unto the Lord; trust also in him; and HE shall BRING IT TO PASS"!*

3. The fact that the Holy Spirit will remind me of God's will for my life.

Jesus said in John 14:26 that the Helper, the Holy Spirit, "*. . . shall TEACH you all things, and BRING ALL THINGS TO YOUR REMEMBRANCE, whatsoever I have said unto you.*" In other words, the Holy Spirit will remind you of God's will for you.

As I already mentioned, prayer is essential to knowing God's specific will for you. And once you are where God wants you to be, and you are doing the things God wants you to do, prayer will *keep* you on the right track.

The things you receive in prayer from the Lord will reveal more of the plan of God for your life and ministry, will warn you of dangers, will warn you of evil men, will show you how to correct, avoid, and overcome problems, and will keep you in the love of God.

Effective praying will make you successful. So maintain your intimate relationship with the Lord!

Living a prayerful life — always talking to Father God — has proven effective for me. But sometimes my wife and I need specific times of prayer to find out some of the specifics for our life and ministry. There are also specific times of prayer when the mission staff comes together each week to pray and talk with God about our missionary work.

The 'How-To's' of Spiritual Preparation

1. *Praying in the Spirit* is a wonderful way to talk to God about the things you don't know how to talk about with your understanding. When you pray in the Spirit, you are speaking forth mysteries, but they're not mysteries to God! He knows what lies ahead, what needs to be done, how to get it done, and what *He* wants to do.

   On the mission field, there are many "unknowns" — things that will vary vastly from your way of life — especially if you are in a new place that's unfamiliar to you. Pray in the Spirit. Pray out of your mouth the will of God concerning the people, your time there, and your ministry to them. Hook up with the Lord. Pray in the Spirit, praying the will of God. Pray in the Spirit in *faith*. An anointing will come upon you, producing supernatural ministry to the people.

2. *Feeding on the Word of God* is another important part of spiritual preparation. Feeding on the Word is not just for preparation, however; it is for spiritual *maintenance*. It is one thing to be able to preach a message for those willing to listen; it's another thing to *live* the message before the people — *all the time*.

   On the mission field, Christians may forgive your shortcomings, but lost people won't! Feeding on the Word of God allows the Word to sink deep into your heart. Putting the Word in your heart on a regular basis develops fine Christian character and brings forth good things from your spirit.

   If you are not careful, wherever you are, but especially on the mission field, you can get too busy. On the mission field, people everywhere need you to come and preach or teach. And over here, as well as in most foreign countries — missionaries are not "a dime a dozen." The last statistic I read said that in Asia, there is only one missionary per 170,000 people! So the need for you to go "everywhere" and minister definitely exists!

   Now if the Lord does want you to go "everywhere," He will show you the "what, where, when, who, and how," so you can accomplish that which He is leading you to do. But He wants you to go to those places spiritually built up and strong, not weak. Prayer and feeding on the Word will help make you spiritually strong. If you omit those two things, then you will always be the one needing someone to come and minister to *you!* But if you are built up — if you are strong in the Lord and in the power of His might — then you can really help and bless someone else.

Design your day, even if you are traveling or ministering for many hours, to have some time to feed on the Word. What would happen to you if you worked hard every day and you quit eating physical food for your body? You wouldn't last long.

In our missions work, we work hard every day. Some days we preach or teach for five hours, sometimes more than that. Some days we only teach for an hour, but with preparing for our seminars and meetings, plus the preparation of tracts, handouts, teachings, and other materials as well as follow-up on the converts, our own paperwork, and personal and family time, time can get away fast. And it *will* get away.

Plus, there is the inconvenience of the lack of modern equipment and poor transportation to deal with. In some nations, everything has to be done underground (in secret), which means it could take much longer to get done.

So if you don't take the time to feed regularly and often on the Word, you will get weak spiritually and become less effective to others, including your family, and to yourself. The mission field is no place for spiritually weak ministers.

3. *Avail yourself of good reference and study books, cassette tapes, and videos.* These things will help you greatly on the mission field. Bring books for your library that cover a wide range of subjects. You can add to those books as time goes by. As a missionary, you will be discipling those you win to the Lord, so you will need to know how to help them in every area of the Word.

Good disciples will produce other new Christians through the witness of their lives and their testimonies. In many places of the world, the Christian witness and testimony is easily seen because the Christian lifestyle contrasts greatly with religion, corruption, traditions, and all kinds of unrighteous lifestyles.

Bring a lot of teaching tapes to the mission field with you. Also, have someone send you tapes on a regular basis. Don't just listen to yourself preach; listen to other proven ministers of the Gospel too.

Listen to tapes of pastors who really speak to *your* heart. Missionaries need good pastoral teaching too. If you don't hear good pastoral teaching yourselves, you can get spiritually "flaky." I have really enjoyed listening to tapes of proven ministers of the Gospel. The ministers we listen to really feed our spirits, correct us, and keep us on the right track. They even feed the vision that we have within us.

Pastoral teaching will help you in discipling others. For example, if you are the only missionary the people have to listen to, and all you preach is salvation and healing, or you can only teach on two or three subjects, both you and your people will be unbalanced. So learn and be *ever learning* from the Word — for your own sake and for the sake of the people to whom God has sent you.

4. *Praise and worship music* is a must for the missionary. You'll have to bring with you the good praise and worship music you may have been used to in your home church, because more than likely, it will not be available in your destination country! Now, instead of your church music

minister, *you* will be the one who will lead others into the praise and worship of God. So bring plenty of music tapes, videos, and song books. You'll need them first for yourself, and then you'll need them to teach the songs to the people.

If a missionary has ever been in your missions area, some of the Christian nationals may know songs you learned 25 years ago in church! Some of those are okay, but you will want to introduce them to a higher and more intimate level of praise and worship. Good praise and worship will also help open people's hearts to receive whatever the Lord wants to give them. God can do great things in the midst of an atmosphere that's been charged by praise and worship. People will come to hear it, and then you can share the Good News!

Consider the fact that you'll be going to people who don't know the Lord at all or who are baby Christians. They usually don't know *anything* about true praise and worship. For example, they might end each song they sing like a rock star ends his song, because they don't know any better! That may have been all they've seen. Or they might play what we call "circus music" with their songs. Or, their songs may be just happy songs that minister to each other's flesh and minds and not to the Lord. So they will have to be taught, and you'll have to teach them. But they can learn, and they *want* to learn.

I look for music and songs that will usher in the Presence of God, the Holy Spirit, and the anointing, and then "maintain" their Presence. For example, on many of my ministry trips, I play certain anointed music tapes to create the right atmosphere for the people to respond to the altar call and to the leading and prompting of the Holy Spirit.

Since no musical group travels with me, I create my own altar-call music to take with me. It works well. I also use anointed music before the service begins to create the right atmosphere and to help prepare the hearts of the people to receive what is ahead. If I'm having an all-day meeting in a village, between services I will play music that "speaks to the hearts," not only as a witness to the lost, but to feed the hearts of the Christians with the love and the power of God.

People in other countries are not used to hearing such anointed music. But they really like it, and they want to play it in their churches and homes. It is a great opportunity to expose the "wonderfulness" of the Father and His Son, Jesus. And the people are charged up and ready to receive before the next service begins!

Reading books and watching teaching videos broadens my knowledge of the Word and shows me ways to better communicate the truths I've learned so that others can learn them. Illustrations, as one of my teachers put it, "are like windows looking into Heaven." Well, I want the Asian people I minister to looking into Heaven all the time!

I sometimes like to dramatize the Word as I'm ministering. I use illustrations, examples, and objects the people can relate to. This opens up the hearts of the people and even causes sinners and religious people to come and hear the wonderful truths I'm sharing.

We have fun, the Holy Spirit is allowed to work in their hearts, and people's lives are changed, enriched, and strengthened. Church becomes a place where the people really are ministered to! They go home with a witness and a testimony. We are constantly exposing the people of this country to the full-Gospel message, and we are training them to do the same for others. Books, tapes, and videos help us to accomplish this task.

Natural Things To Bring to the Mission Field

Good household items are expensive and are generally hard to find on the mission field. Electronics (refrigerators, ranges, radios, stereos, computers) cost two or three times, or more, the price of anything of quality that is imported into a nation. Imported merchandise is still very expensive and selection is limited. All of this makes obtaining certain things you need expensive and time consuming. Our advice is this: Bring what you can afford to bring and what you have room for in your luggage.

We have three children, and the airlines on which we travel allow us to bring two 70-pound suitcases or boxes per person. In those suitcases or boxes, we bring from the States the things we will need for one or two years' time.

Such items include: deodorant, toothpaste, shampoo, vitamins, hair-care items, sheets and towels, clothes, shoes, clothing accessories (ties, belts, purses, and so forth), spices, sauce mixes, flavorings, silverware, pots and pans, house decorations, Post-It note pads, legal pads, glue sticks, Liquid Paper, markers, special paper for office use, the A-Beka Home Video equipment and supplies for our three children (which takes up a lot of space!), Christmas and birthday presents, children's ministry material (teaching aids, books, clip art, puppets, craft materials, and so forth), and ministry materials (books, teaching tapes, music tapes, videos, Bibles, reference books, computer equipment, software, and so forth).

We have to buy these things in the States to bring with us to the mission field because we can't get them where we live in the Philippines. So when we are Stateside traveling and meeting pastors and preaching in churches, we are also spending a lot of time and money on necessary items for our family's future and our ministry. We have to buy these supplies well in advance of their use, but it's fun to go to the stores as a family to buy them. It's like Christmas to us, but it is a very necessary part of being a missionary.

This is an aspect of the missionary life that may seem inconvenient at times. You'll have to buy things well in advance of their use. You'll have to plan. But having the things you need will make you more effective and content. That's so important. It makes living on the mission field a lot easier. Those things — even the "little things" — will greatly minister to you on the field.

Meeting Pastors and Raising Financial Support

On our first trip to the mission field, we were there for two years. Two years is a long time, especially when you are going through all kinds of culture shock! The culture shock does take a while to get over, and some things you will just have to accept. In other words, those things are just the way they always have been, the way they are now, and the way they will be until the people themselves begin to change.

Some things you just have to "swallow" or accept and go on. If you don't learn to deal with things, they will render you ineffective. Culture shock is real. And culture shock coupled with sparse finances will make you want to go home to the States!

We went to the Philippines with only an idea of how much finances we would need per month. We would have been more comfortable and productive if we'd had more money those first two years. But we didn't want to quit; after all, we were just getting started. If we did quit, what were we going to tell the Lord? What else could we do? What excuse could we use to justify leaving the mission field to which God called us?

Having gained valuable missions experience, we were looking forward to itinerating in the States. During our first return trip to the States, I personally met with 38 pastors. I shared with them about our work in the Philippines and about our vision. Most were very impressed, some did not express anything, but only a few of them decided to help us.

To be truthful, we were disappointed. I thought we would really increase our finances during that time. But our finances increased only $600 per month then. However, we've had a steady increase since the beginning, and we've never gone hungry. We've had some really lean months, and we've had some pretty fat months! God has been faithful to us, and through it all, it's been a pleasure serving Him in Asia.

I'm glad to have met all the pastors I've talked with. I've learned many things from meeting each one. After so much time on the mission field, I enjoy meeting pastors who can put something into me, even if it's not finances. I enjoy their friendship and hearing some of their stories about missions work and their own experiences in ministry.

I enjoy being around successful ministers. I like hearing what the Lord has been saying to them. It increases and refreshes me. It ministers life to me. On the foreign field, we are always giving out to people, but back in the States, sometimes pastors give out to me. I like it.

Currently, I return to the States every year. Shelli and our three children will come back every two years. Two years is too long for me to be away from those who support us on the mission field. I really like being with those pastors, churches, and the people who support us. We have a divine purpose and goal that we are fulfilling together! While in the States, I visit other pastors, sharing the vision and the work. I want to give them an opportunity to bring Asians to Christ. Also, I go to whatever meetings RHEMA or Kenneth Hagin Ministries is having at the time. I want to stay on track with the Word and with what God is doing.

But when I return to the States, I spend almost all my time making contacts with pastors. I visit and/or call all my previous contacts. I want to keep our lines of communication open, and I desire their friendships.

One thing more, we depend on our Father God to supply all of our needs. When we meet with pastors, it is just to meet them and to introduce ourselves to them, not to try to extract money from them. We expect that *God* will join certain pastors to us as a result of meeting with them and according to His purpose and plan. We believe God directs churches to give to missions as *He* wills. But meeting these pastors is an important part of missions work for many reasons.

Families on the Mission Field

In the Philippines, we live in a crowded rural town of 60,000-80,000 people. The town is locked in by the mountains and the sea. Yards for children to play in are almost nonexistent. We have not had a yard for four and a half years. Housing is ancient. We just moved into our second house six months ago. Both houses took an incredible amount of remodeling just to get them into shape to live in. They don't build rental houses here, so you have to believe God for a house to become available.

As soon as you can, fix up your house. Make the house into your home. Make it as comfortable as you can make it. Then you'll always have a nice place to which you can retreat every day. If you are uncomfortable in your home, it will affect your ministry. Almost everything can be uncomfortable on the mission field, so your home needs to be a place that ministers to you.

Toys for your children and modern things that you've been used to in the States might not be found where you live on the mission field. There are very few toys in our town, and when we do see them, they are usually of poor quality and very simple. We travel to Manila once or twice a year, but toys are still very limited there. They also cost two or three times the U.S. price if you do find something you'd like to buy. That's why we bring toys and birthday and Christmas presents from the States as much as possible.

Also, few modern appliances and household items are found in our town. You can find some of them elsewhere, but you'll pay two or three times the U.S. price for them. Bring what you can with you. Use your faith to go through customs — it works. Currently, we even have good friends in customs who always help us get through with no problems!

Bring games, books, and videos with you because only in the big cities will you find recreational activities. "Survival" is the word for people in most of the world, so you've got to bring your own entertainment! Living in America, it would be hard to imagine a town without many forms of recreational activities, but it is reality on the mission field.

As a parent, you will need to spend more time with your children on the mission field. Your children will look to you more than ever to supply their needs, especially in the recreational, social, and emotional areas. Actually, that can be a good thing, but you must be prepared for it.

Provide a good education for your children. Sending our children to a boarding school in Manila is not in our plans. We want our children with us, and our children want to be with us. We are a family.

We use the A-Beka home-schooling program for our children. Our children are getting a first-class education at home. The first two years, we used textbooks only. But now our children go to school by video. They get to see other children in class — only they can't communicate with them! The teachers are always excellent, and they explain things really well.

We want our children to prosper in education even on the mission field. It costs less than boarding school, and because of these videos, the children don't lose touch with American children and American ways. A-Beka home schooling is a Christian-based educational program, and we have found that it's good for our children. Since teaching three kids at home can be challenging and sometimes stressful, it is important to establish your heart first in this area.

Our entire family looks forward to opening the mail and "care packages." It's like Christmas! Missionaries get so excited, even over little things that come in the mail. Anything from home puts a smile on our faces. It's nice to know that people remember us. Care packages and letters really do minister to the missionary family. It's so wonderful; it's difficult to articulate how good it really is.

We always emphasize to our children the importance of our work on the mission field. We want them to know that we are doing what God has called us to do. We talk to them about our different meetings and let them know what God did for the people. Our children pray about those meetings and for the people who will be attending. Our children know what we are doing, and they know it is making a difference in the lives of people. Sometimes, but not often, our kids go with us on these ministry trips. They see God at work. When we went to Manila last Christmas, we had only been on the boat for one hour, and Scott Michael, our 11-year-old, had already led five grown men to Jesus!

The last time he took a bus trip with me, coming back from a two-day meeting, he led a man sitting next to him to Jesus. His testimonies always bless the pastors he talks to. Brad, our 10-year-old, prays heartfelt prayers over people at the dinner table, but has not yet led people to Jesus. He does tell me often that he wants to be a preacher just like me. His heart is tender toward Jesus, and it is the same with Brittany, our six-year-old. She loves to sing Christian songs and watch "The Donut Man" on video! The mission field is good for our kids, even with the struggles they go through sometimes.

Fulfilling the Vision

The Bible training center in Catbalogan, Samar, Philippines, is where we teach and train ministers of the Gospel. The students in the school come from all over the nation. This year, we have students from other nations attending. The training center is a full-time, live-in facility. The morning teaching sessions are set up like RHEMA Bible Training Center in the U.S. In the afternoons, students go on daily outreaches to hospitals, jails, and the streets. They also do door-to-door witnessing and conduct weekly Bible studies to disciple the people they lead to Jesus.

These students are being taught and trained how to do the will of God in their lives. They learn how to hear and be led by the Spirit of God. They pray two and a half hours daily. Through the training center, we are able to duplicate ourselves through them, making disciples. Then after all their teaching and training, we send them back to where they came from so they can minister and be a blessing.

Outside of the training center, we conduct all kinds of meetings throughout the Philippines. We have church meetings, multi-church meetings, pastors' and leaders' seminars, crusades, evangelistic meetings, meetings for our alumni, youth meetings, and children's ministry meetings.

We constantly travel to conduct these different meetings for a fourfold purpose: to bring in the harvest, to help people grow up spiritually, to bring revival to the Church, and to strengthen the leadership in the Church.

We prepare teachings, Bible lessons, and other materials for these pastors and leaders. We teach the material first, then leave the leaders the detailed handouts to study. It is making a big difference in this nation!

I spend a lot of time on my computer, typing my sermons, Bible school teachings, Bible lessons, and materials for different kinds of meetings. The printed page is so effective. So many church people in the Philippines don't have a Bible, so when I type up sermons and Bible lessons, I always type the scriptures out. That way the people can continually read the Word along with the commentary that follows. If I can leave the Word in their hands, then the Word can continually speak to them long after I leave.

Also, they use these lessons to teach others. And now that I have put these lessons and teachings on computer, all I have to do is punch a few keys, and the teachings just print out. Then off I go, delivering God's Word on the printed page!

Missions work is absolutely wonderful. Its rewards far exceed this present world. God's grace shines on those called to missions: "The people who sat in darkness *saw a great light,* and upon those who sat in the region and the shadow of death *light has dawned*" (Matt. 4:16).